Culinary Arts Institute®

CARIBBEAN COOKBOOK

CARIBBEAN

CARIBBEAN COOKBOOK

Juliette Hamelecourt

Book designed and coordinated by Charles Bozett
Illustrations by Juliette Hamelecourt
Cover Photo: Bob Scott
Inside Photos: Zdenek Pivecka

COOKBOOK

Culinary Arts Institute®
A DIVISION OF DELAIR PUBLISHING COMPANY

ISBN: 0-8326-0615-4

CONTENTS

CONTENTS

CARIBBEAN CUISINE:

Past and Present

The food habits of the French Caribbean islands have developed slowly since Columbus visited the peaceful Arawak Indians. The primitive Indians were farmers and hunters, and introduced the Spanish settlers to the delights of Caribbean foods. Spanish domination of the islands, with their ruthless genocide of the Indians, ended in 1511 when the majority of the Spaniards went to search for gold in Argentina. The few Spaniards who chose to remain distilled rum along the coast, and also at that time, Father de las Casas, a Spanish priest, brought runaway black slaves to the islands. Spaniards, Indians, and blacks lived in small settlements in peaceful cohabitation. Game, cattle, pigs, and wild horses abounded, there were birds in quantity and paradisiacal vegetation. The islands' small coves and inlets were well shielded from view and were a perfect place for filibusters from France to load food supplies. Some of these filibusters gave themselves to hunting and became known as *boucaniers* from the Carib *boucan*.

Pére Labat, Dominican monk, mathematician, agronomist, expert in artillery, fortification, and also gastronomy, visited the islands in the late 1600's and he thus describes, in his *Voyages aux Isles de l'Amérique*, the food he ate in the house of one of the wealthier buccaneers: "We seated ourselves at the table a little before noon; we could not have been served better than we were—neither with more abundance, order, cleanliness, and delicacy. We were served a breastplate of turtle. This is the whole belly shell of the animal on which has been left three or four fingers of meat and all the fat that can be found there. This fat is greenish and of delicate flavor. The breastplate is placed whole in the oven. It is covered with lime juice, pepper, hot chilies, salt, and ground cloves. The oven should not be hotter than for pastry because turtle meat being tender needs to be cooked with low heat. While the breast is in the oven, pierce it from time to time to spread the juices. Serve it whole—in its shell—cut the steak in thick slices and cover with the rich juices. Never have I eaten anything as good . . ."

Further in his memoirs Pere Labat writes of his visit to a Carib camp: "Fishes had been laid across the fire helter-skelter with the driftwood and some charcoal. At first I mistook the fish for logs, being incapable of imagining any cookery done in so strange a manner. I expressed this feeling to M. La Rose who said these were their ways and that when I had tasted the fish I would find it good and allow the Caribs were not such bad cooks as I imagined . . . . With them we tasted a large scaled fish, the scales coming off like a case, the meat delicious and so rich that one would have thought it had been smeared with butter. True, this fish is fatty, but what has to be remembered is that it is cooked without water, butter or oil to change the substance of its natural juices. This is all for the better. The 'coffre' is a fish covered with a rather thin, dry and hard layer of scales. From its tail to its head joined to the body in one place, it appeared in its entirety like a triangle on the Carib matted table . . . . The smell was good, the meat white and tasty. It was a great pleasure to see this large family of Caribs squatting on their haunches like monkeys and eating without a word with the appetite of abundant health. The women brought in two more tables loaded with freshly baked casava bread with two great hollowed out gourds full of tomalin of crab and *pimentade* (chili sauce). This was accompanied by a large basket of boiled crabs. I have already said that their *pimentade* is so hot that it is impossible for anyone but them to taste it undiluted. I have to make another remark although there is natural salt on the islands, they never use any; they sit there, peeling with great skill and speed the crab legs. They got up with as little ceremony as they had sat down. Those who were thirsty went out to drink water. Some smoked tobacco, others went to their hammocks and the rest entered into a lusty conversation from which I could make nothing since it was in the Caribbean language.

"The women came to take away the tables and the gourd dishes; the maidens cleaned up the place where we had eaten and together with the little children they retired to the kitchen where we went to see them eat with as much appetite in the same posture as the men. I learned from them that except for crabs which form the main part of their food, they never eat anything boiled. Everything is roasted or barbecued. Their way of roasting is to thread the meat on a wooden brochette, to stick it in the ground in front of the fire, and when they feel it is cooked on one side, they give it a turn so the other side will cook; when it is a bird such as a widgeon or a parrot or a chicken they do not even take the trouble to eviscerate it. They throw it in the fire as is. When the feathers are burnt they cover the bird with ash and charcoal and leave it thus, as long as is necessary, after which they take the bird out of the fire, break open the crust which has formed, remove the intestines and the gizzard and eat the bird. I have eaten many times of it. I have always found that the meat rich from its own juices had a great tenderness and admirable delicacy."

Elsewhere: "We then arrived quite late at the buccaneers' settlement where we found three comrades. The camp was in rather a good house, covered with good thatch; and a small smoke house was nearby. Here was a lot of dried meat, other meat which was being barbecued and two or three pigs newly slaughtered. We dined very joyously and with enormous appetite. I had had some wine and eau-de-vie brought in, but my servant had forgotten bread. I ate the buccaneer's boiled plantain instead with the meat, and later the fat and the lean of the pork with *pimentade*. Whether the air, the road or the newness of the situation had given me more appetite than usual or whether the meat was more tender and more appetizing, I think I ate approximately four pounds of it by myself."

At the settler's house, the good father had rail. "The meat of this bird is blackish and smells rather like fish. However it is good and nourishing. The way to cook rail when they are mature, is to throw them into rapidly boiling water and parboil them, after which they must be set to drip. This way of half cooking them takes away the unnecessary fat and the fish smell. Thereupon they are rubbed with bitter orange peel and cinnamon, and roasted." (This must be the original recipe for *canard à l'orange* which Guillaume Tirel, also known as Taillevent, introduced at the Versailles Court a little later.)

Trafficking with pirates was a lucrative business, if somewhat risky. The buccaneers prospered and grew lazy. They brought over from Picardy and Normandy some indentured peasants who tilled for them large tracts of land for seven years before being allowed to become settlers themselves. Pardoned pirates ruled the islands in the name of the King of France. The cultivation of sugar cane, cacao, and coffee replaced the earlier tobacco and indigo. It made the Antilles the richest colonies in the world. Despite careful education by French tutors from France, the descendants of the buccaneers kept a curious kitchen vocabulary sprinkled with galley jargon, the rum habit, and an inimitable way with barbecues. Whether able to travel to France or not, all the planters, says Moreau de St. Mery, who in his books analyzed colonial Haiti with depth and minutiae, talked endlessly of a trip to the mother country "next year." In their desire to make contacts which would be profitable in France, they entertained every passing Frenchman and expended more than they could afford on horses, carriages, and coachmen for the convenience of any visitor who needed go from one end of the colony to the other. To show off their proverbial Creole hospitality, they spent fortunes on their tables, not always in good taste, but always with profusion.

The planter's house was nothing much to look at; spacious, yes, a large square building with a central hall doubling as a dining room. For furniture, nothing but the indispensable. But there were flowers in profusion on his table, servants in shoals, French-trained cooks in numbers. The planter dined gloriously on fresh-water fish from the rivers, rock lobsters from the coral reefs, wild birds from the savannahs. From the cows confined in his *corails*, rich milk was made into cheese for *talmouses*, those golden pâtés, and barbecued suckling pig. The buffet parties, we learn also from St. Mery, were never for less than three hundred people, and the invitations were sent by couriers who rode their horses as if the security of the state depended on their speed. To this day buffets are for three hundred people; houses do not contain much that is considered of value elsewhere; frangipani by the bushel are crowded into perfumed centerpieces on tables laden with fillet of beef, rock lobster with mayonnaise, grillots of pork, *pains au lait*, roast wild turkey, *salaises* and *chiquetailles* of salt fish, heaps of fruit, succulent little pastries, and positively unbelievable cakes turreted and festooned with white icing, and buttercream decorations, dotted with silver seeds and candied fruit.

It has been assumed that the French Antilles serve French food. While it is possible in the restaurants of Martinique, Guadeloupe, and Haiti—and in the elegant homes of their capitals—to eat Parisian meals and drink excellent French wines, the regional cookery of these islands is a blending of many cuisines with a dominant African overtone.

If such restaurants are hard to find, it is because in a country where there is no shortage of household help, there remains a tradition that food is better prepared by one's own cook and eaten at home.

France must attribute its superior restaurants to the fact that after the French Revolution the chefs of titled persons lost their kitchens, and faced with the need of earning a livelihood elsewhere, opened the first and most unique French restaurants on the Continent.

On the Caribbean islands, the basis of all Creole seasoning is hot pepper. There are many varieties of *capsicum frutescens*. Each variety has its lore, its uses: *piment zoizeau* or "bird pepper," so named because it resembles a bird's tongue, is the one we know as cayenne pepper. Martinique has the exclusive *piment zindien*, said to have been the original seasoning of Arawak Indians. *Piment lampio*—Chinese lantern pimento—is also called "billy-goat pimento" because of its strong aroma. It is generally placed unbroken on top of streaming rice so that it can impart its fragrance rather than its strength. Often used unripe and green in stews, it is meant to be slightly acrid. When pink or ripe, it is called *bien parfumé*, and enhances the color of pickles. Cherry pimentos, squat and round, are also named *piment sept court-bouillons*, meaning that it can used seven times. Guadeloupe has *piment bounda manman Jacques*, so voluptuous looking that in Yiddish it might be called "fat woman's tuches."

Besides the fact that pimentos are incorporated whole in certain dishes, these chili peppers also form the basis of a preparation and a method of seasoning which is distinctively Afro-French Caribbean. One of the most typical sounds of the islands is the pounding of *zepices*. From dawn to dark this pounding of spices being reduced to a paste in a mortar echoes in the crystalline air, mingling with the thud of bare feet on hardpan earth in the kitchen compounds, forming a background for the full-throated song of the peasant. Despite the fact that seasoning is based on chili peppers, no one except the newcomer will call the food merely HOT; rather, it is fragrant. There is always, at the base, the French bouquet garni, sea salt, and the elusive taste of lime or sour orange, sometimes both. These small fruit—no bigger than a ping-pong ball—are so abundant that they are used to "wash" fish and meats before cooking.

In the bouquet garni, Caribbean celery is really "lovage," known to all herbalists as the ancestor of the crisp green or white celery we know. It is much stronger in flavor. Garlic is in everything, moderately. The chives, which they call *cives*, is a cross between chives and scallions and is of the garlic family.

The words that are used to name Afro-French Caribbean dishes don't mean what we expect from their regular usage. Bouillons, colombos, daubes, marinades, do not in any way relate to preparations or methods from France. French chefs brought their recipes to the great houses of the colonies in the eighteenth century. Their followers after the Revolution were illiterate cooks, eminently imaginative (as the islanders are today), who named dishes with malaprop inaccuracy and little regard for the orginal French culinary terms.

One of the legacies of French colonialism has been the deforestation of the islands by the coffee planters who believed that the trees would bear better if exposed to sunlight, something which has since been disproved. Gone forever are the magnificent mahogany, rosewood, pine, pallisander, and tulip trees that clothed the mountains. Here and there on the barren mountains and in some villages remain ten- or fifteen-foot-girthed trees: the domain of the spirits around which candles are lit every night and from which no living soul would dare cut even a branch, because in true African animism they link together the world of the living and the dead ancestors—the past, the present, and the future. When these old trees occasionally collapse in a hurricane, their sacred wood is hollowed out and carved into the great ceremonial voodoo drums.

While in Martinique many more modern kitchens exist, in Guadeloupe and in Haiti the charcoal kitchen is still very prevalent, and deforestation continues. To make charcoal the new way is to cut living limbs from a number of species of trees, each having a different use in cooking and all being kindled with slivers of a very resinous pine which also grows in the mountains. As in the Maures region of France, entire villages in the plains are involved in charcoal making. The men set the pits and tend them, the women go side-saddle on their donkeys with a few kilos of charcoal to the special section of the open-air markets.

As in all regional cookery, that of the Antilles is fluid. Each region and each recipe has many variations. Each housewife treasures her own. In making my selection for this book I have often tested and combined ten or more recipes to make one. I have tried not to alter their authenticity by the addition of ingredients foreign to their origin. I do believe that a given culture evolves what is best within a given environment.

Although I have mainly transcribed folk dishes and have indicated the best substitutes available for the few ingredients that cannot be found outside the large cities of the United States, I have also compiled recipes from aristocratic *béké* notebooks, from Creole grandmothers. Desserts are mostly in this category. Confitures, ratafias, and the mélanges have their counterparts in early French cookbooks and also seem to be authentic carry-overs from the eighteenth century. I have enjoyed them as the one sweet thing before the coffee which ends the meal. In the islands I learned again the joyous anticipation of seasonal fruit and vegetables, as opposed to the year-round availability in our frozen food markets. In the Caribbean, April is the month for wild strawberries; May for sugar-loaf pineapples. In midsummer there is a profusion of melons, papayas, and bananas, while June and July are especially noted for many kinds of mangoes. Seasons seem to make meals more exciting. I can remember the pumpkin soup that made my lips tingle with peppery awareness in the Port-au-Prince Iron Market; the dish of millet in a peasant house in Kenscoff where it had been cooked with purslane just weeded out of a field, its tiny cactuslike leaves succulent in the fluffy cereal. In Les Cayes there was *pisquette*—tiny, tiny silvery fish which abound in the delta at certain times of the year; and another time, the boiled turtle eggs eaten one evening at Ibo Beach under an indigo sky.

So many pleasant meals I remember, and all the friends with whom I shared them during a three-month visit to the Caribbean which turned into a ten-year stay.

GLOSSARY

acra (akkra)—vegetable fritters

amber rum—rum which is aged in charred, oaken barrels, imparting an amber color and resulting in a fuller flavor; can be used interchangeably with light rum

ancienne, à l'—old-fashioned way

Antilles—name for a group of islands in the Atlantic Ocean, presently known as the West Indies, except in France where Guadeloupe and Martinique form the Department of Les Antilles

Barbancourt rum—popular medium-bodied Haitian rum, produced since 1862

bouquet garni—a bunch of aromatic herbs used to flavor soups, stews, braised dishes, and sauces. Usually made with 3 or 4 parsley sprigs, 1 thyme sprig, and ½ bay leaf, tied neatly together; celery may also be added. Enclose fine, dry herbs in a cheesecloth bag; remove before serving.

breadfruit—a tropical tree which produces a large, round, starchy fruit which is eaten before it is ripe and sweet; may be baked, boiled, or fried

chayote—tropical fruit prepared like summer squash

chipolata sausage—small Italian sausage which may be baked, fried, or grilled

clarified butter—pure butter fat lacking browning characteristics and used in sauces and baked goods. Obtained by melting butter over low heat, then chilling it. Discard the top and bottom layers.

court bouillon—herb-and-vegetable-flavored liquid used as an ingredient for various dishes or to poach fish

crawfish (crayfish)—small shellfish similar to lobster and cooked in the same manner

Creole à la—main dish served with rice pilaf and garnished with sweet peppers and tomatoes

croutons—bread slices or small cubes fried in butter until crisp

curaçao—orange-flavored liqueur

deglaze—to loosen pan drippings with wine, stock, or other liquid

dried Italian pepper pods—small, dried red peppers

flan—baked custard

friture—French word for fried foods

génoise—a moist cake similar to a rich sponge cake

ginger beer—slightly alcoholic, ginger-flavored beverage

granadilla—three varieties of this fruit: Sweet Granadilla, Passion Fruit, and Granadilla Giant. Sweet Granadilla and Passion Fruit are eaten fresh or used in cakes, jellies, and ice cream. Granadilla Giant resembles watermelon in appearance, but its flavor is inferior compared to the other varieties.

guava—tropical fruit with sweet flavor which is eaten raw or stewed; used in jams and jellies

guinea fowl—small bird with delicate flesh prepared like chicken

hot pepper—available fresh or canned; often called cayenne or bird pepper

kirsch—cherry brandy

light rum—clear, light bodied, and dry; its flavor is not as robust as amber rum

Madeira—sweet wine from Madeira Island in the Atlantic Ocean, used as a beverage and also in sauces; available sweet, semidry, and very dry

malanga—tropical root vegetable prepared like potatoes; its leaves, callaloo, are used in soups

mango—tropical fruit which is used in preserves when green and unripe. When ripe and red the yellow flesh is sweet and juicy. Available April through September.

meunière—foods, especially fish, cooked in melted butter, lemon juice, and parsley

mortar—strong bowl in which herbs, spices, and other foods are crushed with the aid of a pestle

orgeat—sweet syrup made from almonds and used in beverages

ortolans—small bird with delicate flavor; prepared like other game birds

palm hearts—tender vegetable obtained from the top of palm trees

papaya leaves—used to tenderize meats and poultry

because it contains the enzyme papain

plantain—banana-like fruit. When unripe (green) they are less sweet and are cooked before eating; fully ripe (dark brown) plantains are sweet and tender enough to be used raw, as in salads.

port—sweet, dessert wine available as ruby, tawny, or white

poulet—French word for chicken

ratatouille—mixture of eggplant, sweet peppers, tomatoes, and zucchini sautéed in oil; served hot or cold

roulade—slice of meat rolled around a filling

saffron—expensive spice made from the dried stigmas of an autumn-flowering crocus; should be used sparingly in bouillabaisse, curries, and rice dishes

sorrel—tropical herb; leaves used in salads and soups or as a vegetable; the flower is used in drinks, jams, and sauces

soursop—tropical fruit often used for juice and ice cream

tamarind—tropical tree; its fruit is a pod containing compressed seeds surrounded by pulp, used in beverages and marmalade

tournedos—a fillet steak cut from the tenderloin wrapped with pork fat or bacon and secured

truffles—a rare edible fungus which when cooked adds a delicate flavor to other foods; some varieties are eaten uncooked

velouté—rich white sauce similar to béchamel sauce; used as a foundation for more elaborate sauces

15

APPETIZERS

As in eighteenth-century Paris, around the capitals of the French-speaking Antilles, near the provincial open markets or at crossroads, is to be seen a special breed of pipe-smoking, leather-faced ambulant cook. By trade, she is the descendant of the French *friturière*, greengrocer. Squatting on her heels, her skirt modestly brought forward diaperwise, she seems to be staring vacantly at the smoke rings she makes, unconcerned about her pots and her charcoal burner. She arrived on the job at five in the morning, at the first cock's crow (the *kirikiki*), carrying the whole load on her head in the inverted burner. Her helper is dispatched to the market stalls to purchase beans, rice, oil, yellow cornmeal, plantains, hot peppers, herbs and pork casings, sausage meat, and cubed pork. After that, the round-bottomed pots will be scrubbed inside, rinsed many times, and polished with steel, until the cooking begins. When the food is ready, should the first customer be a woman, the *friturière* will pretend not to see her, and should the woman be so rude as to insist, will angrily chase her away no matter how affluent she may look. But if the first customer is a man, she will greet him with a smile, fuss over the food, and select the tenderest piece. *Gasson ce chance*, "men bring luck," and this will be a profitable day.

A *friturière* uses enough fat for the food to float in, and she makes it really hot but not smoking. She is careful to keep a separate pot for fish frying. She does not have a food thermometer but she knows that the fat is hot enough to fry with when a slice of plantain or bread rises to the surface immediately when thrown into the hot fat and browns before she has counted to fifty. She knows also by experience that too many pieces of food will reduce the temperature of the fat, so she fries only a little at a time.

Her wares, when made in the home kitchen, are delicious too. They can be prepared in larger portions and served as a main course with an accompaniment of rice and beans.

Deep-Fried Plantain

Green plantain
Ice water
Peanut oil for deep frying, heated to 365°F
Salt

1. Peel plantain; reserve the skin. Slice the plantain on the slant in 2½-inch pieces. Soak in water.
2. Without draining, drop a few pieces of plantain into the oil. Fry for 2 minutes. Remove, using a spoon with a long handle. Repeat until all pieces are fried.
3. Place a fried plantain piece inside the reserved skin. Press between the palms of the hands to flatten the fried plantain; the edges will be jagged. Remove from skin and deep-fry again until golden brown. Flatten and refry all pieces. Drain on absorbent paper. Sprinkle with salt and serve hot.

Pasties *(Pâtes Chauds)*

1 cup ice-cold water
1 teaspoon salt
3 cups all-purpose flour
1¼ cups vegetable shortening
Cold milk (about ¼ cup)
Beef Filling (½ recipe)
1 egg yolk, beaten

1. Combine water and salt. Place flour in a large mixing bowl and make a well in the center. Pour salted water into well and mix lightly with a spoon without kneading. Place dough in refrigerator 30 minutes.
2. Roll the dough into a rectangle ¼ inch thick. Spread half the shortening on the dough. Fold one side over the middle and spread this section with the remaining shortening. Fold over the remaining section and again roll out to ¼-inch thickness. Fold again into thirds and roll out. Repeat this rolling process a third time. Refrigerate dough overnight.
3. Roll the dough to about ½-inch thickness. Cut the dough into 2½-inch rounds. Roll out trimmings to cut more rounds.
4. Place a tablespoonful of filling in the center of half the dough rounds. Brush the edges with milk. Cover with remaining rounds, lightly pressing the edges down. Brush the tops with egg yolk. Place pasties on a baking sheet with sides. Place a pan of hot water on the bottom rack of the oven.
5. Bake at 400°F 30 minutes, then turn the oven control to 300°F and bake 20 minutes, or until golden brown.

1 dozen

Beef Filling

2 parsley sprigs
¼ small green hot pepper or 6 dried Italian pepper pods
2 shallots, chopped
1 garlic clove
½ pound ground beef, cooked
1 cup Béchamel Sauce (page 62; use beef broth)

1. In a mortar, pound to paste the parsley, pepper, shallot, and garlic.
2. Add seasoning paste and cooked beef to Béchamel Sauce; mix well.

Note: Half of the filling is needed for Pasties; use remainder for hot sandwiches or as desired.

Filling may also be made with leftover cooked chicken, fish, tongue, ham, or mushrooms. Follow above procedure, using chicken or fish broth in Béchamel Sauce.

Pork Tidbits *(Grio)*

2 pounds pork loin
½ orange
½ lime
Salt, pepper, and garlic to taste
2 cups water
½ cup bacon drippings
Ti-Malice Sauce (page 62)
Deep-Fried Plantain (page 16)

1. Remove bones from pork loin and cut meat into small cubes, keeping all the fat on the meat. Rub meat first with the cut side of orange, then with cut side of lime. Season with salt, pepper, and garlic.
2. Put the meat and water into a Dutch oven and cook covered over high heat until all water has evaporated, leaving the fat only.
3. Add bacon drippings to meat in Dutch oven and fry meat over medium heat, stirring occasionally, until meat is brown and crisp.
4. Heap meat on a round platter, sprinkle generously with sauce, and surround with plantain pieces.

Meatballs with Breadfruit

1 breadfruit (about 1 pound)
1 garlic clove
1 teaspoon lime juice
1 tablespoon chopped chives
2 parsley sprigs
3 eggs
1 cup cooked ground meat
½ cup finely ground peanuts
   Oil for frying, heated to 365°F
   Tomato Sauce Creole (page 63)

1. Peel breadfruit. Boil about 20 minutes in salted water, or until soft; drain. Mash as for potatoes.
2. In a mortar, pound to a paste the garlic, lime juice, chives, and parsley. Combine paste with mashed breadfruit, 2 eggs, and cooked ground meat; beat until fluffy. Roll into walnut-size balls; coat with beaten egg and then peanuts.
3. Fry in heated fat until golden. Drain on absorbent paper. Serve hot with the sauce as a dip.

Note: Breadfruit may also be combined with ham, poultry, game, salt cod, or salt herring.

Meatballs à l'Haitienne

4 white bread slices
1 cup milk
1 pound freshly ground lean beef
2 slices smoked ham or bacon, minced
   Salt and pepper to taste
1 garlic clove, crushed in garlic press
1 tablespoon tomato paste
½ cup flour
½ cup grated Parmesan cheese
   Fat for frying, heated to 365°F
   Tomato Sauce Creole (page 63)

1. Soak bread in milk 5 minutes, then mash and mix with ground beef, minced ham, salt, pepper, garlic, and tomato paste. Roll into walnut-size balls; coat with flour and then with cheese.
2. Fry in heated fat until golden brown. Drain on absorbent paper. Serve hot with the sauce as a dip.

Note: These meatballs may be made larger for a main course and are usually served with Cornmeal (page 60) and a salad.

Cocktail Puffs (Marinades)

1 tablespoon coarse salt
2 peppercorns
1 scallion or green onion, cut in pieces
2 parsley sprigs
⅛ teaspoon ground mace
1 teaspoon lime juice
4 drops Tabasco
1 cup all-purpose flour
1 tablespoon baking powder
2½ cups water
1 egg yolk
1 cup chopped cooked calf's brains, chicken, turkey, smoked herring, shrimp, lobster, or fish
2 egg whites, stiffly beaten
   Peanut oil for frying, heated to 365°F

1. In a mortar, pound to a paste the salt, peppercorns, scallion, parsley, mace, lime juice, and Tabasco.
2. Sift flour with baking powder into a bowl. Mix in water, seasoning paste, egg yolk, and desired cooked ingredient. Fold in beaten egg white.
3. Pour the batter by tablespoonfuls into the heated fat; it will spread. Gather the batter with a circular motion as it floats on top of the fat and looks like a wafer. Fry until crisp, golden, and lacelike. Drain on absorbent paper. Serve hot.

Chicken Fritters Guadeloupe

2 cups minced cooked chicken
3 tablespoons finely chopped parsley
2 tablespoons finely chopped chives
3 tablespoons fresh bread crumbs
1 tablespoon grated onion
1 tablespoon curry powder
   Salt to taste
¼ teaspoon cayenne or red pepper
¼ cup Dijon mustard
½ cup dry bread crumbs
1 egg, beaten with 1 teaspoon
      peanut oil
   Oil for frying, heated to 365°F

1. Mix chicken with parsley, chives, fresh bread crumbs, onion, and seasonings. Shape mixture into walnut-size balls, roll in dry bread crumbs, then in beaten egg, and again in bread crumbs. Chill in refrigerator.
2. Just before serving, fry in hot oil until golden brown. Drain on absorbent paper and serve hot.

Eggplant Fritters

3 long thin eggplants
1 tablespoon lime juice
   Salt, pepper, and cayenne or
      red pepper to taste
1½ cups all-purpose flour (about)
¾ cup beer (about)
   Oil for deep frying,
      heated to 365°F
   Salt

1. Slice eggplants into eighteen ½-inch rounds. Season with lime juice, salt, and ground peppers. Marinate 15 minutes.
2. Make a batter the consistency of whipping cream by mixing flour with beer.
3. Dip and coat eggplant slices in batter. Fry in heated oil until golden brown. Drain on absorbent paper. Sprinkle lightly with salt. Serve hot.

Artichoke Fritters: Follow recipe for Eggplant Fritters. Substitute **artichoke hearts** or **bottoms** for eggplant rounds.

Corn Fritters

1 cup fresh corn kernels
½ cup butter
1 cup all-purpose flour
4 eggs
   Corn oil for frying,
      heated to 365°F

1. Cook corn until soft in boiling salted water in a saucepan; drain thoroughly, reserving 1 cup liquid. Melt butter with corn liquid in saucepan, add flour, and cook, stirring rapidly, until mixture is smooth and rolls away from the sides of pan.
2. Remove from heat and add the eggs, one at a time, beating well after each addition. Stir in cooked corn.
3. Drop batter by spoonfuls into heated oil and fry until golden and well puffed. Drain on absorbent paper. Serve hot.

Acra

5 dried Italian pepper pods or
      1 small piece hot pepper
1 tablespoon coarse salt
6 peppercorns
½ medium onion, chopped
2 garlic cloves
1 egg
1 cup finely grated malanga root*
   Peanut oil for frying,
      heated to 365°F

1. In a mortar, pound together to a paste the pepper pods, salt, peppercorns, onion, and garlic.
2. Add seasoning paste and egg to grated malanga root; beat until light.
3. Drop mixture by spoonfuls into heated oil and fry until golden. Drain on absorbent paper.

20 fritters

*Malanga root can be found in Puerto Rican markets.

Codfish Fritters

½ pound salt cod
3 dried Italian pepper pods or
    1 very small piece hot pepper
2 garlic cloves
2 green onions, cut in pieces
2 parsley sprigs
2½ cups all-purpose flour
1 teaspoon baking powder
1 cup light beer
    Peanut oil, heated to 365°F
    Dilled Avocado Sauce for Fish
      (page 63)

1. Soak cod in cold water overnight. The next day, drain the cod, add fresh water, and bring to a boil. Drain, cool, and shred finely.
2. In a mortar, pound together to a paste the pepper pods, garlic, onion, and parsley.
3. Sift flour with baking powder into a bowl; stir in beer. Add the seasoning paste and shredded cod; mix well.
4. Drop batter by teaspoonfuls into heated oil. Fry until golden. Drain on absorbent paper. Serve hot with the sauce.

Haitian Rarebit

8 kaiser rolls
16 slices American or Cheddar cheese
½ cup sweet pickle relish
1 cup chopped cooked ham, chicken,
    beef, or tongue
8 tablespoons butter or margarine,
    melted

1. Split rolls. On bottom half of each roll, place in the following order: 1 slice cheese, 1 tablespoon sweet pickle relish, 2 tablespoons chopped meat, and another slice cheese. Replace top of roll.
2. Generously brush top and bottom of sandwiches with melted butter.
3. Place rolls in a large skillet over medium heat. Cover with a lid slightly smaller than the skillet and weight it down over the rolls. Brown both sides until cheese melts. Serve immediately.

8 servings

Shrimp Paste à la Creole

    Fresh shrimp
    Court Bouillon for Fish and
      Shellfish (page 30)
¼ cup butter, melted
1 garlic clove, crushed in a
    garlic press
⅛ teaspoon ground mace
⅛ teaspoon pepper
    Tabasco to taste

1. Cook enough shrimp in bouillon to make 4 cups shelled shrimp.
2. Put shrimp, hot melted butter, garlic, mace, pepper, and Tabasco into container of an electric blender; process 10 seconds.
3. Serve on **toasted cassava** or **Melba toast**.

Oysters Barquettes Gourmet Club Port-au-Prince

Pastry (see Turnovers Aquin, page 21)
1 jar pickled oysters, drained
¾ cup Béchamel Sauce (page 62; use fish broth)
1 cup coarsely chopped artichoke hearts
Finely shredded Swiss cheese

1. Prepare pastry, roll out, and cut to fit barquette or other small molds. Press dough firmly into molds against bottom and sides. Prick with a fork. Fill with beans or lentils, if desired.
2. Bake at 375°F 12 minutes. Pour out beans, if used. Unmold and set aside.
3. Measure 1 cup oysters; reserve remainder for garnish.
4. Combine sauce, artichoke hearts, and 1 cup oysters. Spoon mixture into barquettes and sprinkle with cheese. Glaze under a broiler; top each with an oyster. Serve hot.

Turnovers Aquin

Aquin is a small town in the south of Haiti renowned for its mangrove oysters.

1½ cups all-purpose flour
¼ teaspoon salt
⅓ cup peanut oil
2 tablespoons ice-cold water
1 jar pickled oysters
Milk for brushing
Peanut oil for deep frying, heated to 365°F

1. For pastry, combine flour and salt in a bowl. Mix in oil and ice-cold water. Gather dough into a ball and roll out very thin between 2 sheets of waxed paper. Cut out 3-inch rounds with cookie cutter or inverted glass.
2. Slightly off center on round, place 3 oysters. Fold in half, coming to within ¼ inch of the opposite edge. Moisten rim with a pastry brush dipped in milk. Fold rim back over itself to seal.
3. Fry in heated fat until golden. Drain on absorbent paper.

Salt Cod Salad (Mor Marinée)

1 pound dried cod fillet
3 peppercorns, cracked
1 whole clove, cracked
⅛ teaspoon nutmeg
5 dried Italian pepper pods or 1 small hot pepper
1 sweet pepper, cored, seeded, and julienned
4 shallots, chopped
2 garlic cloves, crushed in a garlic press
1 cup olive oil
¼ cup wine vinegar
¼ cup chopped mixed chives and parsley
Biscuits Port-au-Prince (page 60)

1. Put cod into a sieve and slowly pour 2 quarts very hot water over it. Shred fish and remove all bones and skin. Add peppercorns, clove, nutmeg, pepper pods, julienne of pepper, shallots, and garlic; mix well. Add olive oil and vinegar; mix again. Marinate 3 days in refrigerator.
2. Mound marinated mixture on a serving platter. Sprinkle with mixture of chives and parsley. Serve on halved hot buttered biscuits.

Peppery Peanut Butter and Coconut Sandwiches

8 slices white bread
6 tablespoons peanut butter
2 tablespoons butter, softened
1 teaspoon Tabasco
½ cup freshly grated or chopped
     flaked coconut

1. Remove crusts from bread. Flatten each slice with a rolling pin and cut into 3 strips.
2. Combine peanut butter, butter, and Tabasco.
3. Spread peanut butter mixture on bread; dip in coconut. Roll each bread strip to form a pinwheel.
4. Chill thoroughly before serving.

2 dozen appetizers

Avocado Cocktail Dip

1 large ripe avocado
2 teaspoons lemon juice
1 small slice onion
¼ cup mayonnaise
6 drops of Tabasco
   Salt to taste
   Potato chips

1. Halve and peel avocado, reserving 1 shell. Cube avocado and put into container of an electric blender. Add lemon juice, onion, mayonnaise, Tabasco, and salt. Process until puréed.
2. To serve, pile avocado mixture into reserved shell; place on a serving dish and surround with potato chips for dipping.

About 1 cup

SOUPS

Panades, or bread soups, are eaten by the country people in the morning. *Gombos, gros bouillons, soupe à Congo* and *calalou* were the food of the slaves after the return from the fields. While in peasant homes plain water is used for making soup, I urge you to use good stock, broth, or consommé as a base, as this will vastly improve these soups. Adding an envelope of gelatin to 2 cups of broth brings it closer to consommé texture.

The *gombos* of Haiti have okra as a base and are given their black color by *djon-djons,* a species of tree mushroom unavailable in the United States, which when made into a tea will render a black juice. It is a dish which rarely can be savored in North America but certainly must be partaken of on a trip to Haiti.

The *gombos* of Guadeloupe and Martinique, also called *calalou,* are made from the leaves of four different tropical plants and are also very rarely to be tasted here.

Vivres alimentaires, root crops, some of which were imported from Africa by the planters, some of which were native to the islands, form the basis and the thickening for the *gros bouillons.* Most of these can be found in southern states and in the Puerto Rican markets of many of our cities.

Bouillon Cocq

This soup is traditionally served on Christmas Eve when the family and guests return from midnight mass.

1 **meaty smoked ham hock**
1 **capon (7 to 8 pounds)**
½ **lime**
½ **orange**
2 **tablespoons bacon drippings**
1 **tablespoon butter**
1 **tablespoon peanut oil**
3 **quarts water**
   Bouquet garni
1 **pound cabbage, cut in chunks**
4 **small potatoes, pared and**
       cut in chunks
2 **carrots, pared and cut in chunks**
2 **white turnips, pared and**
       cut in chunks
2 **onions studded with**
       8 whole cloves
2 **celery stalks, cut in pieces**
2 **leeks, washed and cut in chunks**
   Salt, pepper, and cayenne or red
       pepper to taste
   Caribbean Rice (page 59)

1. Soak ham hock in cold water to remove excess salt. Drain.
2. Truss capon as for roasting. Rub skin with cut side of lime half, then cut side of orange half. Let stand to drain.
3. Heat bacon drippings, butter, and peanut oil in a deep soup kettle. Brown capon. Add ham hock, water, and bouquet garni; bring to a boil, reduce heat, and simmer 30 minutes, skimming twice.
4. Add vegetables and seasonings, bring to a boil, skim, then cook over low heat 30 minutes, or until vegetables and meats are tender.
5. Put the capon on a large platter and surround with drained vegetables and rice. Drink the broth from cups.

Breadfruit Soup Guadeloupe

1 **breadfruit (about 1½ pounds)***
2 **bacon slices, fried and crumbled**
4 **cups Coconut Milk (page 86)**
2 **tablespoons soft butter (optional)**

1. Bake breadfruit at 350°F 45 minutes. Open it and remove the center; peel and dice the meat. Put breadfruit, bacon, and Coconut Milk in a bowl. Purée a little at a time in an electric blender or in a food mill, adding butter if necessary. Heat.
2. Serve in bouillon cups and garnish with **toasted grated coconut.**

*Breadfruit can now be found in many supermarkets and most Puerto Rican markets.

Consommé with Oxtails

3 tablespoons olive oil
1 medium oxtail (about 4 pounds)
8 large tomatoes, peeled and seeded
2 medium onions
2 quarts beef broth
  Freshly ground pepper
  Coarse salt
1 large garlic clove, crushed in a
    garlic press
  Sprig fresh basil or ⅛ teaspoon
    dried basil
1 cup sliced carrot
1 cup fresh peas
4 plantains, boiled

1. Heat oil in a soup kettle. Add oxtail and cook until well browned.
2. Mince tomatoes and onions together. Add to meat in kettle, reduce heat, and simmer 3 minutes. Add broth and seasonings. Cook uncovered 1½ hours, then add carrot and peas; continue to cook until meat easily comes from the bones.
3. Serve consommé with a piece of meat and a plantain half in each soup plate.

8 servings

Congo Soup (Gros Bouillon Habitant)

3 tablespoons lard
3 pounds beef shin bones
1 pound lean beef for soup
  Marrow bone
3 quarts water
2 tablespoons coarse salt
1 teaspoon ground pepper
8 dried Italian pepper pods or
    1 green hot pepper, pricked
3 carrots, pared and cubed
3 leeks, washed and cubed
3 parsnips, pared and cubed
3 plantains, peeled and cubed
12 shallots, halved
4 cups cubed pumpkin
1 pound cabbage, cut in chunks
1 pound malanga root or rutabaga,
    peeled and cubed
  Handful spinach or sorrel leaves
2 tablespoons tomato purée
¾ cup cooked rice

1. Heat lard in a large soup kettle. Add shin bones, soup beef, and marrow bone and brown to a rich golden color. Add water and bring to a boil. Add salt, ground pepper, and pepper pods. Simmer covered 45 minutes, skimming soup twice.
2. Add remaining ingredients except spinach, tomato purée, and rice; simmer covered 40 minutes, or until vegetables are tender.
3. Remove bones and meat. Slice marrow and cube the meat; reserve.
4. Press vegetables against side of kettle with the back of a large wooden spoon. Add spinach and cook 5 minutes, then stir in tomato purée.
5. Spoon 1 tablespoon cooked rice in center of each soup plate and pour in soup.

12 servings

Pumpkin Bread Soup (Panade of Pumpkin)

4 garlic cloves
1 green hot pepper or
    6 dried Italian pepper pods
4 cups beef broth
4 slices white bread
2 tablespoons peanut oil
1¼ cups minced onion
1 can (16 ounces) pumpkin or
    1 pound pared and cubed
    fresh pumpkin (see Note)
¼ pound spinach leaves

1. Put garlic and hot pepper into a mortar and pound to a paste. Set aside.
2. Pour beef broth over bread; set aside.
3. Heat peanut oil in a large saucepan; sauté onion. Add bread with beef broth, pumpkin, and seasoning paste; mix well. Simmer 10 minutes.
4. Add spinach; bring to boiling, reduce heat, and cook 5 minutes.

About 1½ quarts

Note: If fresh pumpkin is used, process the soup in an electric blender before adding the spinach.

Purée of Malanga Soup

3 tablespoons peanut oil
1 bunch scallions or green onions, minced
3 pounds malanga root, peeled and diced
2 quarts rich stock
Salt, black pepper, and cayenne or red pepper to taste
⅛ teaspoon nutmeg
1 garlic clove, crushed in a garlic press
Bouquet garni
Few celery leaves
Fresh basil sprig

1. Heat peanut oil in a soup kettle. Add minced scallions and cook until translucent but not brown. Add malanga root, stock, and seasonings and cook until malanga root is tender.
2. Purée through a food mill or in an electric blender.
3. Serve with **toasted white bread**.

About 12 servings

Creamy Fresh Tomato Soup

2 shallots
1 tablespoon coarse salt
1 large garlic clove
8 peppercorns
8 large tomatoes, peeled, seeded, and quartered
2 quarts beef broth or rich stock
1 small beet, pared
1 cup uncooked rice
1 cup whipping cream
½ cup chopped mixed parsley and chives

1. In a mortar, pound shallots, salt, garlic, and peppercorns to a paste.
2. Put tomato quarters into a soup kettle and add broth, seasoning paste, and beet. Cook 12 minutes, then add rice, bring to a boil, reduce heat, and cook 30 minutes.
3. Purée tomato-rice mixture in an electric blender or force through a food mill. Return to kettle, bring to a boil, and stir in cream.
4. Serve in soup cups and sprinkle with parsley and chive mixture.

Cream of Turnip Soup

¼ cup peanut oil
½ cup minced onion
6 medium white turnips, pared and quartered
1½ quarts chicken broth
Marrow bone
Bouquet garni
Salt and pepper to taste
3 dried Italian pepper pods or 1 whole pink hot pepper
1 cup whipping cream

1. Heat oil in a soup kettle. Add onion and cook over low heat until translucent but not brown, stirring constantly. Add turnips, broth, marrow bone, and seasonings; bring to a boil, reduce heat, and cook 30 minutes. Remove marrow bone and pepper pods. Slice bone marrow thinly and set aside.
2. Purée turnip mixture in an electric blender or force through a food mill. Return to kettle, add cream, and stir to blend. Bring to boiling point.
3. Serve garnished with **avocado cubes**, **red sweet pepper strips**, and reserved bone-marrow slices.

Note: This soup can also be served iced, but then omit the bone marrow which will congeal and be unappetizing.

Head Soup

1	veal, pork, or lamb head
2	limes, halved
¼	pound salt pork
6	dried Italian pepper pods or 1 green hot pepper
2	garlic cloves
5	parsley sprigs
1½	to 2 quarts chicken broth or stock
4	tomatoes, peeled, seeded, and quartered
3	carrots, pared and cut in chunks
2	onions, cut in chunks
2	leeks, washed and cut in chunks
2	plantains or green bananas, peeled and cut in chunks
2	purple yams, pared and cut in chunks
1	parsnip, pared and cut in chunks
2	cups cubed pared pumpkin
½	cup corn kernels
½	pound lima beans
¼	pound cabbage, cut in chunks
	Bouquet garni
	Pepper to taste
	Caribbean Rice (page 59)

1. Have your meat man trim the head and prepare it with the tongue separated. Rub the head with cut sides of lime halves, squeezing gently and going into all cavities.
2. Render the salt pork in a small skillet over low heat.
3. Meanwhile, in a mortar pound the pepper pods, garlic, and parsley to a paste.
4. Pour the fat from the salt pork into a large soup kettle, add the head, tongue, and seasoning paste (no salt is needed). Pour in enough broth to cover, bring to a boil, skim twice, reduce heat, and simmer 1 hour.
5. Add vegetables and seasonings; bring to a boil and simmer until vegetables are tender and meat comes from the bones. Remove the bones and meat. Cut meat into pieces.
6. Crush the vegetables against side of kettle with a spatula, potato masher, or large wooden spoon.
7. Serve in soup plates with a generous portion of meat and a small mound of rice in each.

Velouté Martinique

1	cup crab meat from boiled crab
1	cup fish broth from a fish head or boiled crab
2	chicken breasts
2	tablespoons olive oil
1	cup water
	Bouquet garni
3	dried Italian pepper pods
1	cup Coconut Milk (page 86)

1. Have crab meat and broth ready.
2. Sauté chicken breasts in oil until golden. Add water, bouquet garni, and pepper pods; cover and simmer until chicken is tender. Remove chicken and reserve liquid.
3. Cut the chicken into small pieces; add crab meat, reserved liquid, fish broth, and Coconut Milk. Purée, a little at a time, in an electric blender.
4. Serve hot in soup cups and garnish with **grated coconut**.

Pickled Oyster Stew

1	cup milk
1	jar pickled oysters, drained
¼	cup peanut oil
½	pound onions, minced
	Salt and freshly ground pepper to taste
1½	quarts stock
2	egg yolks
1	cup whipping cream

1. Pour milk over oysters and let stand 2 hours.
2. Meanwhile, heat oil in a soup kettle. Add onion and cook slowly until translucent but not brown. Season with salt and pepper and add stock; cook 30 minutes.
3. Beat egg yolks with cream and set aside.
4. Drain oysters, rinse with water, and pat dry on absorbent paper. Add to the stock and bring to a boil. Immediately stir in cream-egg mixture and remove from heat.
5. Serve from a tureen and sprinkle each serving with **freshly ground pepper** and **cayenne** or **ground red pepper**.

Fisherman's Soup (Bouillon Pecheur)

1 pound each halibut, whiting, sea
    trout, and red snapper
    Juice of 1 lime (reserve halves)
    Juice of 1 orange
    Salt and pepper to taste
1 pound shrimp
8 small crabs
1 small lobster
1 pound conches removed from
    shells
    Meat tenderizer
4 garlic cloves
5 parsley sprigs
5 scallions or green onions,
    cut in pieces
8 dried Italian pepper pods or
    1 pink hot pepper
1 tablespoon coarse salt
¼ cup peanut oil
12 shallots
8 small potatoes, pared and cut
    in chunks
4 onions, sliced
3 carrots, pared and cut in chunks
3 plantains, peeled and cut in chunks
1 chayote, cut in chunks
1 leek, washed and cut in chunks
1 parsnip, pared and cut in chunks
1 yam, pared and cut in chunks
1 pound pumpkin meat, cut
    in chunks
½ pound malanga root, peeled and
    cut in chunks (optional)
3 quarts water
1 cup amber rum
12 slices white bread with crusts
    removed, fried

1. Cut fish into serving pieces and put into a shallow dish. Season with lime juice, orange juice, salt, and pepper; let stand 30 minutes.
2. Shell and devein shrimp; rub crabs and lobster with pieces of lime. Set aside.
3. Rinse shelled conches in many waters. Sprinkle them with meat tenderizer and beat them with a meat hammer to make them soft. Cut into strips. Set aside.
4. In a mortar, pound to a paste the garlic, parsley, scallions, pepper pods, and salt.
5. Heat oil in a large soup kettle. Sauté onion, adding the seasoning paste, until mixture is golden but not brown. Add conch strips, vegetables, water, and rum; bring to a boil, then reduce heat and simmer 30 minutes. Add lobster and crabs; cook 10 minutes. Add fish and cook 10 minutes, then add shrimp and cook 5 minutes.
6. With a wooden spoon or potato masher, press some of the vegetables against side of kettle. Remove lobster and cut into serving pieces.
7. Put fried bread into deep soup plates and add the soup.

12 servings

Snapper Chowder à l'Ancienne

4 pounds red snapper fillets
    Juice of 1 lime
    Salt, freshly ground pepper, and
    cayenne or red pepper to taste
8 tomatoes, peeled and seeded
5 scallions or green onions
2 tablespoons soybean or peanut oil
    Court Bouillon for Fish and
    Shellfish (page 30)
2 cups potato balls
1 cup diced carrot
1 cup diced turnip
8 bread slices, fried

1. Drizzle fish with lime juice and season with salt and peppers. Set aside.
2. Chop tomatoes and scallions together finely.
3. Heat oil in a large saucepan, add tomato-scallion mixture, and cook slowly until mixture is like a liquid paste. Add bouillon and bring to a boil. Add vegetables and cook 20 minutes.
4. Cut fish into small portions, add to saucepan mixture, and simmer 7 minutes, or until fish flakes.
5. To serve, spoon chowder over fried bread in soup plates.

8 servings

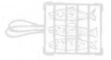

FISH AND SHELLFISH

The waters of Guadeloupe and Martinique are rather lacking in fish. People say this has been the case since the eruption of the volcano Mount Pelée at the turn of the century. The fish must have fled to Haiti, where the tropical varieties in their rainbow colors are brought in on the wings of the trade winds between 1:00 and 2:00 P.M. and netted by a flotilla of dinky sailboats. Fish is sold right on the shore in Martissan: the small ones impaled on a stick called *corde* or "string"; the large ones resting on a bed of dark seaweed.

Inland people cannot possibly bring fresh fish from the sea to their homes under the blazing sun. They rely on the meager catch in mountain streams or they buy imported salt cod and Canadian alewives—hard, salt, smoked kipper fillets.

Court Bouillon for Fish and Shellfish

1 onion
1 leek
1 carrot
3 celery stalks
5 parsley sprigs
1 basil sprig
2 tablespoons olive oil
2 quarts boiling water
  Bouquet garni
6 peppercorns, cracked
2 whole cloves
6 dried Italian pepper pods or
  1 whole pink hot pepper
½ cup amber rum

1. Finely chop fresh vegetables and herbs together.
2. Heat oil in a large saucepan, add chopped mixture, and cook until lightly browned. Add boiling water, bouquet garni, peppercorns, cloves, pepper pods, and rum. Cover; boil 30 minutes. Boil uncovered to reduce volume by half.
3. Strain and cool before using.

About 1 quart

Scrambled Eggs with Salt Cod

5 parsley sprigs
2 green onions, chopped
1 garlic clove, crushed in a
  garlic press
1 dried Italian pepper pod or
  1 sliver green hot pepper
1½ cups shredded soaked salt cod
3 tablespoons peanut oil
1 cup hot milk
6 eggs

1. In a mortar, pound together to a paste the parsley, onion, garlic, and pepper pod. Mix this seasoning paste with the shredded cod.
2. Heat oil in a skillet, add fish mixture, and brown it, adding hot milk.
3. In another skillet, scramble eggs to a soft consistency while gradually adding the fish mixture.

4 servings

Stuffed Fish Odette Mennesson

1 large grouper or bluefish
  (4 to 5 pounds)
  Court Bouillon for Fish and
  Shellfish (page 30)
6 hard-cooked eggs
2 cups Herbal Mayonnaise Odette
  Mennesson (page 64), chilled
1 cup crab meat
  Parsley
  Lime wedges and avocado slices
  for garnish

1. Have the fish split and boned without removing the head or tail.
2. Bring court bouillon to boiling in a large roasting pan. Wrap fish in cheesecloth and put into pan, leaving the ends of the cloth out of the pan. Poach 7 to 10 minutes, or until fish is thoroughly cooked.
3. Meanwhile, mash eggs with mayonnaise; mix in crab meat.
4. Gently remove fish from bouillon and transfer from cloth to a platter. Spoon crab mixture between the two halves of fish. Serve warm, or if desired, chill thoroughly.
5. To serve, arrange parsley around fish and garnish with slices of lime and avocado.

Stuffed Red Snapper

1 red snapper (about 5 pounds)
  Salt and pepper to taste
½ lime
¼ cup flour
1 cup cooked rice
1 cup chopped raw shrimp
½ cup chopped green onion
    (including top)
½ cup very thinly sliced celery
1 tablespoon grated ginger root
2 bacon slices
¼ cup dry white wine

1. Season red snapper inside and out with salt and pepper. Rub with cut side of lime. Sprinkle evenly with flour.
2. Combine rice, shrimp, onion, celery, and ginger root. Spoon into fish; skewer or sew the opening. Lay fish in a very heavily buttered baking pan. Score the top of fish in an attractive design to prevent it from buckling. Lay bacon slices over top.
3. Bake at 350°F 45 minutes, or until fish flakes. Transfer fish to a heated platter.
4. Deglaze baking pan with white wine. Pour liquid over fish.

Red Snapper à l'Orange

1 red snapper (5½ to 6 pounds)
  Salt and cayenne or red pepper
    to taste
  Juices of 1 lime and 1 orange
  Court Bouillon for Fish and
    Shellfish (page 30)
  Bouquet garni
16 potato balls
16 small carrots, cut in chunks
6 leeks (white part only), halved
8 unpeeled orange slices
3 tablespoons tomato paste
  Saffron Rice (page 59)

1. Season red snapper with salt, cayenne, and juices; allow to marinate 30 minutes.
2. Pour court bouillon into a fish steamer. Place the fish in steamer along with bouquet garni, vegetables, and orange slices. Simmer uncovered on top of the range or bake at 450°F 20 minutes.
3. Transfer fish carefully to a heated platter. Arrange the vegetables around it. Garnish with orange slices.
4. Measure 2 cups fish broth and blend with tomato paste; pour over vegetables. Serve with the rice.

Red Snapper Meuniere

2 red snappers (2 pounds each)
2 limes, halved
  Salt and pepper to taste
½ cup flour
  Peanut oil (about ¼ cup)
  Butter (about 2 tablespoons)
5 drops Tabasco
¼ cup butter
1 tablespoon chopped parsley
1 tablespoon lime juice
  Lime wedges for garnish

1. Have the fins and tails trimmed from fish, without removing the heads. Rub the fish with cut side of lime halves, squeezing gently to release the juice. Season with salt and pepper. Superficially slash the skin of the fish in a diamond design.
2. Put flour into a bag large enough to hold fish; put fish into bag and coat them evenly with flour.
3. Heat enough oil and butter to cover the bottom of a skillet large enough to hold both fish. When fat is sizzling, add Tabasco. Sauté fish about 12 minutes on each side, or until done, reducing the heat if necessary so as not to scorch them.
4. Meanwhile, cream ¼ cup butter with parsley.
5. Remove fish to a heated plater and keep warm. Discard all the fat in bottom of the skillet and add butter with parsley and the lime juice; stir until blended. Spoon over fish.
6. Garnish platter with lime wedges.

6 servings

Macadam of Cod Martinique

2 pounds salt cod
¼ cup olive oil
2 large onions, chopped
⅛ teaspoon cayenne or red pepper
Bouquet garni
1 garlic clove, crushed in a garlic press
3 tomatoes, peeled, seeded, and cut in chunks
1 tablespoon olive oil
1 teaspoon lime juice
¼ cup chopped parlsey
Caribbean Rice (page 59)

1. Soak cod in cold water overnight. The next day, drain, trim edges from fish, and coarsely shred fish.
2. Heat ¼ cup oil in a large skillet. Add onion and cod; cook until lightly browned. Add pepper, bouquet garni, garlic, and tomato; mix well. Cook covered over low heat 15 minutes. Add 1 tablespoon oil and the lime juice; mix well.
3. Transfer cod mixture to a serving platter and sprinkle with parsley. Serve with the rice.

Eggplant and Salt Cod (Morue e Beregenes)

2 pounds salt cod
1 eggplant (2 pounds), pared and sliced
½ cup olive oil
2 garlic cloves, crushed in a garlic press
5 drops Tabasco
1 tablespoon tomato paste
Bouquet garni
Juice of ½ lime
Salt and pepper to taste
French-Fried Breadfruit or Deep-Fried Plantain (pages 52, 16)

1. Soak cod in cold water overnight. The next day, place the fish in a sieve and slowly pour 1 quart boiling water over it. Bone fish, trim, and remove any skin, then shred and set aside.
2. Cook eggplant slices in salted water 3 minutes, then drain.
3. Put oil, garlic, Tabasco, and tomato paste into a Dutch oven; mix. Add reserved fish, the eggplant, and bouquet garni. Cook over medium heat until eggplant falls apart. Mix in lime juice, salt, and pepper.
4. Serve hot with breadfruit.

Crab Zoumba: Follow recipe for Eggplant and Salt Cod, substituting **2 pounds crab meat** for cod.

Guadelupean Blaffe

2 pounds salt cod
3 garlic cloves
⅛ teaspoon cayenne or red pepper
10 parsley sprigs
3 peppercorns
3 scallions or green onions, cut in pieces
3 celery leaves
1 fresh dill sprig or ⅛ teaspoon dried dill
2 quarts water
Bouquet garni
Caribbean Rice (page 59)

1. Soak cod in cold water overnight. The next day, drain cod and reserve.
2. In a mortar, pound together to a paste the garlic, cayenne, parsley, peppercorns, scallions, celery leaves, and dill.
3. Bring water to boiling in a soup kettle. Add the seasoning paste and bouquet garni; bring to a boil. Add reserved cod and simmer until the cod flakes.
4. Serve in soup plates with the rice.

Cod Casserole

1 pound salt cod
12 small potatoes
12 small onions, peeled
3 tablespoons olive oil
⅛ teaspoon cayenne or red pepper
Black pepper
½ cup half-and-half

1. Soak cod in cold water overnight. The next day, drain and then rinse under running cold water.
2. Cook cod, potatoes, and onions separately in water, adding no salt. Drain when tender.
3. Remove all bones from cod, trim edges from fish, and cut into 2-inch pieces. Place fish in alternating layers with onions and potatoes in a top-of-range casserole. Drizzle with olive oil, sprinkle with cayenne and black pepper, and pour half-and-half over all. Cover and simmer over low heat 20 minutes.
4. Serve cool, but not cold, with a green salad.

Cod Soup *(Chaudrée of Cod)*

1 pound salt cod
¼ pound salt pork, cubed
1 tablespoon chopped onion
2 sprigs celery leaves
4 parsley sprigs
4 peppercorns, cracked
1 shallot, halved
¼ cup tomato paste
4 drops Tabasco
Bouquet garni
1 cup potato balls
1 quart stock
Boiled Plantain (page 53)

1. Soak cod in cold water overnight. The next day, put cod in a sieve and gently pour 1 quart boiling water over it. Flake cod and reserve.
2. Sauté salt pork and onion in a soup kettle until light brown. Set aside.
3. In a mortar, pound together to a paste the celery leaves, parsley, peppercorns, and shallot.
4. Add seasoning paste to kettle along with tomato paste, Tabasco, bouquet garni, potato balls, flaked cod, and stock; stir. Bring to a boil, reduce heat, and simmer gently until vegetables are tender.
5. To serve, put plantain into soup plates and add soup.

Barbecued Crabs

8 large hard-shell crabs
½ lime
Creole Barbecue Sauce (page 63)
Caribbean Rice (page 59)

1. Rinse crabs in water several times. Rub the shells with the cut side of a lime half, squeezing a little to release some of the juice. Cut off the heads just behind the eyes and discard the green sac; lift the belly apron and cut it away, too.
2. Put the crabs in a hinged grill and barbecue 5 inches away from glowing coals for about 5 minutes on each side. Immediately brush with the sauce.
3. Serve crabs with the rice.

8 servings

**Pepper Steak Port-au-Prince 38
with Smothered Mixed Vegetables 57**

Crab Meat Omelet Martinique
(Omelette aux Ouassous)

3 tablespoons butter or margarine
1 package (6 ounces) frozen crab
    meat, thawed, drained,
    and flaked
2 teaspoons finely chopped onion
2 teaspoons chopped parsley
¼ cup dairy sour cream
1 tablespoon dry sherry
4 eggs
2 tablespoons water
    Salt and pepper to taste

1. For filling, melt 1 tablespoon butter in a skillet. Add crab meat, onion, and parsley; heat thoroughly. Stir in sour cream and sherry. Set aside.
2. For omelets, beat eggs in a bowl; add water, salt, and pepper.
3. In a small skillet, melt 1 tablespoon butter over high heat. Add half the beaten eggs. Immediately use a fork or spoon to push the edges of the thickened egg mass towards the center; the liquid will immediately fill the vacant spaces. Repeat this procedure until the eggs are cooked but still soft. Remove from heat.
4. Place half the crab filling in the middle of the omelet. Fold the omelet in thirds to enclose the filling.
5. Repeat procedure for making an omelet, using the remaining beaten eggs and crab meat filling. Serve immediately.

2 omelets

Lobster Canapé

6 rock lobster tails
    (at least ½ pound each)
    **Court Bouillon for Fish and
    Shellfish (page 30)**
9 tablespoons olive oil
6 tablespoons butter
16 white bread slices with crusts
    trimmed
2½ cups Béchamel Sauce (page 62)
2 egg yolks
⅓ cup amber rum, warmed and
    flamed
¾ cup chopped cashews
2 tablespoons chopped parsley
1 tablespoon chopped dill

1. Cook lobster tails in court bouillon until tender; drain, reserving bouillon. Slice lobster into chunks ½ inch thick.
2. Heat 3 tablespoons oil and 2 tablespoons butter in a large skillet. Add a few bread slices and fry until golden, turning once. Repeat frying procedure with more oil, butter, and bread slices. Set croutons aside and keep hot.
3. Prepare Béchamel Sauce with the reserved bouillon; blend in egg yolks and rum. Mix in lobster pieces. Keep warm in a chafing dish.
4. Sauté cashews in 2 tablespoons butter; stir in parsley and dill.
5. To serve, spoon lobster mixture onto croutons and sprinkle with herbed cashews.

Barbecued Eel

1 eel (about 3 pounds)
2 garlic cloves
1 scallion or green onion,
    cut in pieces
4 dried Italian pepper pods
1 basil sprig
3 parsley sprigs
2 peppercorns
1 tablespoon coarse salt
¼ cup lime juice
1 cup peanut or olive oil
1 cup cornmeal

1. Have eel skinned and cleaned; cut into 3-inch chunks.
2. In a mortar, pound together to a paste the garlic, scallion, pepper pods, basil, parsley, peppercorns, and salt. Blend lime juice and oil into seasoning paste. Pour over eel chunks and marinate overnight.
3. When ready to barbecue, pour cornmeal into a bag, add chunks of eel, and shake to coat. Place eel in a hinged grill and barbecue 5 inches from ash-covered coals, basting frequently with the marinade; turn pieces so they brown on both sides.
4. Serve with Creole Barbecue Sauce (page 63) or Ti-Malice Sauce (page 62) and **barbecued yams** (see Yams and Sweet Potatoes, page 58).

Haitian Rock Lobster Salad

8 rock lobster tails
Court Bouillon for Fish and
   Shellfish (page 30)
4 cups Caribbean Rice (page 59)
16 cherry tomatoes, washed and
   stemmed
1 cup cubed pared cucumber
3 celery stalks, diced
1 cup cubed fresh pineapple
1 cup small Greek black olives
¼ cup capers
1 cup French Dressing Antillaise
   for Salads (page 64)
4 hard-cooked eggs, peeled and
   quartered
¾ cup amber rum

1. Simmer lobster tails in court bouillon 20 minutes. Belly side down on a board, split the tail lengthwise with a sharp knife and keep warm in the bouillon until serving time (see Note).
2. Toss rice with vegetables, pineapple, olives, and capers. Add dressing and toss again.
3. Mound the rice mixture on a large silver platter, garnish with hard-cooked egg quarters, and edge platter with drained cooked lobster tails.
4. At the table, warm rum, ignite it, and pour it flaming over the lobster.

8 servings

Note: If you have room in the freezer, save the court bouillon to use as a base for Béchamel Sauce for fish or for a chowder.

Crawfish or Jumbo Shrimp au Gratin Guadeloupe

50 small crawfish in their shells or
   50 shelled raw jumbo shrimp
   Court Bouillon for Fish and
   Shellfish (page 30)
3 tablespoons butter
1 tablespoon peanut oil
1 pound sliced calf's liver
6 mushrooms, sliced
1 tablespoon chopped parsley
⅛ teaspoon dried marjoram
⅛ teaspoon dried rosemary
   Salt, freshly ground pepper, and
      cayenne or red pepper to taste
3 white bread slices with crusts
   trimmed
1 egg, beaten
½ cup dried bread crumbs
½ cup finely shredded Swiss cheese
½ cup whipping cream
2 tablespoons amber rum, warmed
   and flamed

1. Cook crawfish in boiling court bouillon 10 minutes, then cool. Reserve 1 cup bouillon.
2. Heat butter and oil in a skillet; sauté liver and mushrooms until liver is firm on the outside and pink inside. Season with parsley, marjoram, rosemary, salt, and peppers.
3. Soak bread slices in reserved bouillon; stir to break up bread. Process soaked bread with bouillon and liver-mushroom mixture, a little at a time, in an electric blender or force through a food mill. Stir in egg.
4. Spread mixture on bottom of a shallow baking dish. Arrange crawfish decoratively on top. Sprinkle with a mixture of bread crumbs and cheese. Blend cream and rum; pour over all. Broil until lightly browned.

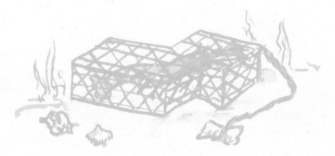

Dr. Gagneron's Fish in Pastry

1   cup cold water
1   teaspoon salt
2   cups all-purpose flour
½   cup butter
1   grouper (about 2½ pounds)
    Court Bouillon for Fish and
    Shellfish (page 30)
1   cup Béchamel Sauce (page 62;
    made with strained court
    bouillon)
12 raw oysters, shelled
¼   cup capers
½   cup chopped red and green sweet
    peppers
    Milk

1. For pastry, chill a bowl and pastry board. Combine water and salt. Put flour into the chilled bowl, make a well, and pour in the salted water; mix without kneading. Refrigerate dough 30 minutes.

2. Roll the dough into a rectangle ¼ inch thick on chilled and floured pastry board. Lightly trace lines dividing the rectangle into 3 even sections.

3. Spread the butter on the middle section, working quickly. Fold the 2 sides over the middle. Roll again to ¼-inch thickness. Fold into thirds and roll again. Fold into thirds and refrigerate overnight.

4. For filling, poach grouper in court bouillon. When the fish flakes at the touch of a knife near the backbone, remove from broth. Cool and shred it, discarding the skin and bones.

5. Combine sauce, the shredded grouper, oysters, capers, and peppers. Set aside.

6. Roll pastry to ¼-inch thickness. Spread the filling on half the pastry; fold the other half over it. Brush the edges with milk and press to seal. Brush the top surface with milk. Put on a baking sheet with sides.

7. Bake at 400°F 30 minutes; turn oven control to 350°F and bake 15 minutes, or until pastry is browned.

MEAT, POULTRY, AND GAME

Juliette

Mountain animals and those that roam the countryside are perforce lean and develop a tougher musculature. Thus the native meats of the islands have a tendency to be tough. Meat, poultry, and game have to be treated to be tender. Nature has provided the means: In every backyard or in the marketplace can be found a papaya or a bitter orange tree. The leaves of the one and the juice of the other provide natural tenderizers. Papaya leaves can be used fresh or strung up in a sunny window, dried to brittleness, and pounded to powder in a mortar. The powder is then stored in a glass jar with a tight-fitting cover.

Variety meats are plentiful and cooked mostly according to French recipes. Sweetbreads, the thymus gland of calves, are imported. The supply of game birds is rich: moorhens, woodcocks, teal, and snipe; wild guinea hen, widgeons, quail, egrets, herons, turtledoves, and ortolans, their full-flavored meat a welcome change from poultry raised in ultra-modern chicken farms. In the tropical climate they are best cooked soon after they are shot. Rabbit, farm raised, many be purchased, it is best stewed in the Parisian style.

Whatever the meat, the seasoning will be a perfectly blended symphony of herbs and spices, the robust simplicity of the dishes exalted by the meticulous care lavished on their preparation. The methods of cooking the different game birds are really interchangeable.

Pan-Fried Steak

⅓ cup prepared mustard
1 beef boneless sirloin steak
    (4 pounds)
¼ cup lard
1 onion, minced
2 cups beef stock
½ teaspoon beef extract or
    1 beef bouillon cube
1 teaspoon tomato paste
2 tablespoons butter
2 tablespoons cornstarch
    Salt and pepper to taste

1. Spread mustard on all sides of meat.
2. Melt lard in a large, heavy skillet and sauté onion. Add meat and brown well on all sides. Reduce heat and continue to cook until the meat is done. Transfer to a warm platter and keep hot.
3. Remove fat from skillet. Pour in stock to deglaze; add beef extract and tomato paste.
4. Mix butter and cornstarch and put into skillet juices. Stir constantly over medium heat until sauce is slightly thicker. Add salt and pepper.
5. Pour a little sauce over the meat. Serve remaining sauce in a sauceboat. Garnish meat with Smothered Mixed Vegetables (page 57).

Pepper Steak Port-au-Prince
(Steak au Poivre Port-au-Prince)

2 tablespoons peppercorns
8 beef sirloin steaks (4 pounds),
    about 2 inches thick
2 tablespoons peanut oil
2 tablespoons butter
1 onion, minced
    Salt to taste
½ cup dry white wine
¼ cup beef stock
3 tablespoons butter
2 tablespoons chopped parsley
¼ cup amber rum

1. In a mortar, pound the peppercorns until coarsely crushed. With the heel of the hand, press peppercorns into the meat.
2. Heat oil, 2 tablespoons butter, and onion over high heat in a large skillet. Sauté steaks in the fat until meat is as done as desired. Season with salt. Transfer meat to a warm platter and keep hot.
3. Pour wine and stock into the skillet over high heat to deglaze. Add the remaining butter and parsley. Pour mixture over the meat.
4. Warm rum, ignite it, and pour it, still flaming, over the steak.
5. Serve immediately with Smothered Mixed Vegetables (page 57).

8 servings

Broiled Beef with Barbecue Sauce

1 beef boneless sirloin steak,
    1 inch thick (about 4 pounds)
½ cup prepared mustard
    Pepper to taste
    Creole Barbecue Sauce (page 63)
5 tablespoons butter
2 tablespoons chopped parsley
2 tablespoons chopped chives
    Salt to taste

1. Lay beef on a broiler rack and spread mustard over surface. Score meat deeply in a diamond pattern. Season with pepper. Brush Creole Barbecue Sauce over meat.
2. Broil 4 inches from heat 6 to 8 minutes on each side, or until as done as desired. When meat is turned, brush with the barbecue sauce.
3. While meat cooks, combine butter, parsley, and chives. Set aside.
4. Place meat on a hot platter and season with salt. Spread butter mixture over meat. This will melt and mix with meat juice. Serve with French-Fried Breadfruit (page 52) and Caribbean Rice with Bean Sauce (pages 59, 65).

8 to 10 servings

Vegetable-Smothered Steak *(Filet Touffé)*

8 beef loin tenderloin or boneless
    sirloin steaks (about 4 pounds),
    cut thin
3 garlic cloves
2 parsley sprigs
1 thyme sprig
1 teaspoon coarse salt
2 tablespoons prepared mustard
1 tablespoon orange juice
1 cup sliced carrot
1 cup shredded cabbage
4 medium onions, sliced and
    separated in rings
3 large truffles, sliced
¼ pound ham, cubed
¼ pound salt pork, cubed
    Madeira or port wine
    (about 1 cup)
¾ cup amber rum
    Beef stock
2 tablespoons butter
2 tablespoons cornstarch
    Salt and pepper to taste

1. Pound steaks until flattened.
2. In a mortar, pound to a paste the garlic, parsley, thyme, and salt. Add mustard and orange juice to the seasoning paste.
3. Combine carrot, cabbage, onion, truffles, ham, and the mustard mixture. Set aside.
4. Render salt pork in a skillet. Remove the cracklings and add to the vegetable mixture. Brown the steaks in the fat over medium heat.
5. Alternate layers of the steak and vegetable mixture in a large casserole with a tight-fitting cover. Pour wine into the casserole dish to fill it one third full.
6. Warm the rum, ignite it, and pour it, still flaming, over the meat. Cover casserole tightly.
7. Bake at 450°F 20 minutes, then turn oven control to 325°F and continue to cook 4 hours.
8. Transfer steaks and vegetables to a warm platter and keep hot.
9. Measure liquid in casserole and add enough beef stock to equal 2 cups. Pour liquid into a saucepan and set over medium heat.
10. Mix butter and cornstarch and add to liquid in saucepan. Stir constantly until thickened. Add salt and pepper.
11. Pour sauce over meat or serve in a sauceboat. Accompany with Purée of Breadfruit (page 52).

Tournedos Caribbean

8 beef tenderloin steaks
  (about 4 pounds)
½ cup prepared mustard
  Freshly ground pepper to taste
2 tablespoons butter
8 goose liver slices (¼ inch thick)
  Flour
½ cup beef stock
1½ teaspoons beef extract or
  3 beef bouillon cubes
⅓ cup amber rum
2 tablespoons butter
2 tablespoons cornstarch

1. Pound steaks until about 1 inch thick. Spread mustard on one side of each steak. Roll up steaks with mustard side in and secure with string. Season with pepper.
2. Melt butter over medium heat in a heavy skillet. Coat liver with flour and sauté until golden brown on both sides. Transfer liver to a warm dish and keep hot.
3. Place steak rolls in skillet and cook until as done as desired. Add more butter if necessary.
4. Arrange the steak rolls on a warm platter and place a sautéed liver slice on each one.
5. Pour the stock and beef extract into skillet to deglaze. Warm the rum, ignite it, and pour it, still flaming, into the skillet.
6. Mix butter and cornstarch and add to liquid in skillet. Bring to a boil, stirring constantly; remove from heat and pour over steak rolls.
7. Serve immediately with French-Fried Breadfruit (page 52).

8 servings

Beef Stew

¼ cup peanut oil
1 large onion, thinly sliced
3 to 4 pounds beef boneless chuck
  or rump, cubed
2 cups beef stock
1 can (10½ ounces) tomato purée
  Bouquet garni
1 green hot pepper or
  6 drops Tabasco
  Salt and pepper to taste
3 cups diced potato
3 cups cubed white turnip
3 cups sliced carrot
  Water
2 tablespoons butter
2 tablespoons flour
1 tablespoon chopped parsley

1. Heat oil in a Dutch oven; sauté onion until golden brown, stirring constantly. Add meat and brown on all sides.
2. Add beef stock, tomato purée, bouquet garni, hot pepper, salt, and pepper; stir to blend. Cover and simmer over low heat 2 hours, or until meat is tender.
3. Add potato, turnip, and carrot. If more liquid is needed, add water. Bring to a boil and simmer 20 minutes, or until vegetables are tender.
4. Discard the bouquet garni and hot pepper. Transfer meat and vegetables to a warm platter.
5. Combine butter and flour to make a paste; add to pan juices and boil until thickened. Add parsley, and, if desired, salt and pepper.
6. Pour gravy over meat and vegetables. Serve with Coconut and Rice and Smothered Cabbage (pages 59, 56).

8 to 10 servings

Note: Lamb or kid may be substituted for the beef.

Scallop of Kid or Veal
(Escalopes de Cabrit ou de Veau)

16 small kid or veal scallops,
  (about 3 pounds)
2 eggs, beaten
2 tablespoons vegetable oil
1 teaspoon lime juice
  Salt and pepper to taste
  Dry bread crumbs
2 tablespoons butter
2 tablespoons vegetable oil

1. Cut meat into pieces the size of a silver dollar, then pound between 2 sheets of waxed paper until very thin.
2. Mix eggs, 2 tablespoons oil, lime juice, salt, and pepper. Dip each piece of meat into the egg mixture, then in the bread crumbs.
3. Heat remaining butter and oil in a skillet over medium heat. Sauté the meat until golden brown on each side. Add more butter and oil to skillet if necessary.
4. Serve with Rice and Avocado (page 59).

8 servings

Braised Shanks

8 lamb shanks
1 cup cubed salt pork
½ cup each peas, coarsely chopped onion, sliced green beans, cubed white turnip, and sliced carrot
1 cup boiling water
½ cup dry white wine
7 peppercorns
3 parsley sprigs
1 thyme sprig
1 garlic clove
1 teaspoon salt
½ cup red wine
¾ cup beef broth
1 tablespoon butter
1 tablespoon cornstarch
1 tablespoon chopped parsley

1. Thoroughly wash shanks in cold water; drain. (If necessary, pull off the parchmentlike covering.)
2. In a Dutch oven render the salt pork, and in this fat sauté the shanks over high heat until brown on all sides.
3. Remove Dutch oven from heat; add vegetables, water, and white wine.
4. In a mortar, pound to a paste the peppercorns, parsley, thyme, garlic, and salt. Add to the shanks. Bring to a boil over high heat.
5. Remove Dutch oven from heat and add red wine and ½ cup beef broth.
6. Cook covered in a 375°F oven 2 hours.
7. Mix butter and cornstarch. Set aside.
8. Transfer shanks to a large serving platter; arrange vegetables around shanks.
9. Pour ¼ cup beef broth into Dutch oven to deglaze and place over high heat. Add butter mixture and stir constantly until thickened. Pour into a serving dish and sprinkle with parsley.
10. Serve with Caribbean Rice and Bean Sauce (pages 59, 65).

About 4 servings

Note: Beef, veal, or kid shanks may be substituted for lamb shanks.

Veal Roulades

6 veal cutlets (1½ pounds)
½ cup peanut oil
2 large onions, chopped
½ cup fresh bread crumbs
¼ cup chopped parsley
½ teaspoon salt
½ teaspoon freshly ground pepper
1 egg yolk, beaten
¼ cup butter
1 cup stock
12 small onions
12 small carrots
1 green hot pepper or 5 dried Italian pepper pods
1 tablespoon butter
1 tablespoon cornstarch

1. Pound the meat until flattened. Set aside.
2. Heat oil in a small skillet and sauté the chopped onion. Add bread crumbs, parsley, salt, and pepper; stir to blend. Remove from heat and stir in egg yolk. Cool.
3. Spread some of the mixture on each piece of meat. Roll up the slices of meat and secure with string.
4. Melt ¼ cup butter in a large skillet and brown the roulades. Add stock.
5. Simmer covered over low heat or cook in a 375°F oven about 2 hours, or until tender; add onions, carrots, and pepper halfway through cooking.
6. Transfer meat and vegetables to a warm platter and keep hot. Discard pepper.
7. Mix butter and cornstarch and put into skillet juices. Stir constantly over medium heat until sauce is slightly thicker. Pour sauce over roulades.
8. Serve with Caribbean Rice (page 59).

6 servings

Ham Rolls Guadeloupe

¼ cup amber rum
2 cups Béchamel Sauce (page 62;
    use beef broth)
8 ham slices
    (about ¼ inch thick)
1½ cups Creamed Spinach

1. Add rum to Béchamel Sauce. Pour sauce into a skillet and add ham slices; heat thoroughly.
2. Transfer ham, a slice at a time, to a baking dish, place 3 tablespoons Creamed Spinach on each slice and roll up. Secure with picks, if necessary. Pour sauce in skillet over ham slices.
3. Broil 4 inches from heat about 5 minutes, or until warmed and glazed.
4. Serve with Bananas à l'Antillaise (page 53).

8 servings

Creamed Spinach: Chop 1½ cups cooked spinach very fine. Season with **salt** and **pepper** to taste. Melt **1 tablespoon butter** and stir in **1 teaspoon flour**. Add ½ **cup milk** and cook 3 minutes, stirring constantly. Add chopped spinach and heat thoroughly.

Calf's Liver with Basil

1½ pounds calf's liver, cut in strips
½ cup flour
    Salt and pepper to taste
½ cup butter
2 garlic cloves
1 tablespoon minced onion
½ cup beef stock
1 teaspoon dried basil
2 tablespoons butter
1 tablespoon cornstarch

1. Coat liver strips in a mixture of flour, salt, and pepper.
2. Melt butter in a skillet over medium heat. Add garlic, onion, and liver strips. Sauté meat 3 minutes on each side. Transfer the meat to a warm platter and keep hot.
3. Deglaze the skillet with the stock; add basil. Mix butter and cornstarch and add to the stock. Cook and stir mixture until slightly thickened. Pour over liver.
4. Serve liver with Sweet Potato Soufflé (page 56).

4 to 6 servings

Ragout of Brains

2 pounds calf's brains
6 peppercorns
5 shallots, halved
4 parsley sprigs
1 small carrot, cut in pieces
1 teaspoon salt
¼ teaspoon thyme
¼ cup butter
2 tablespoons soybean oil
¼ cup beef stock
1 tablespoon tomato paste
2 tablespoons butter
1 tablespoon lime juice

1. Remove membrane and blood from brains, then soak brains in cold water for 30 minutes. Simmer for 15 minutes in water. Drain and drop into cold water.
2. In a mortar, pound to a paste the peppercorns, shallots, parsley, carrot, salt, and thyme.
3. Melt ¼ cup butter with oil in a medium skillet. Add the brains and seasoning paste. Sauté, gently stirring, until the meat is golden.
4. Add stock and tomato paste; cook 5 minutes longer, then add the remaining butter and lime juice.
5. Serve immediately with Deep-Fried Plantain (page 16).

About 8 servings

Beef Liver à la Beauharnais

½ cup flour
1 tablespoon paprika
½ teaspoon salt
⅛ teaspoon freshly ground pepper
⅛ teaspoon cayenne or red pepper
1½ pounds beef liver, thinly sliced
1 cup minced onion
3 tablespoons peanut oil
2 tablespoons butter
1 tablespoon chopped parsley
1 tablespoon lime juice

1. Combine flour, paprika, salt, and peppers. Coat liver slices with flour mixture. Set aside.
2. Sauté onion in oil over medium heat. When onion is translucent, add butter and liver slices. Cook liver about 5 minutes; do not overcook.
3. Arrange liver on a heated platter and sprinkle with parsley and lime juice. Garnish with **watercress**.

6 servings

Beef Tongue King Christophe

1 fresh beef tongue (about 4 pounds)
Water
1 carrot
1 onion stuck with 4 cloves
½ cup lime juice
Bouquet garni

1. Wash tongue and put into a large saucepan. Add water to cover and remaining ingredients. Cover and simmer about 2 hours, or until tongue is tender.
2. Cool tongue, then remove skin; cut away roots and gristle.
3. Slice the tongue diagonally and against the grain. Arrange slices on a platter. Garnish with sliced **hard-cooked eggs, pickles, avocado wedges,** and **sliced tomatoes**.

About 12 servings

Tripe à la Creole

2 pounds tripe
1 lime, halved
Water
1 tablespoon coarse sea salt
1 tablespoon wine vinegar
4 garlic cloves
1 green hot pepper or
   3 dried Italian pepper pods
½ cup olive oil
2 large Spanish onions, sliced
1 cup cubed cooked ham
5 large tomatoes, peeled, seeded, and chopped
¼ cup amber rum
2 thyme sprigs
2 bay leaves

1. Wash tripe thoroughly in cold water; drain. Rub the cut surface of lime over entire tripe. Put into a large kettle, cover with water, and add salt and vinegar. Bring to a boil; simmer 5 hours, adding more water if necessary. (This step is generally done the day before tripe is served; tripe is left to cool in its water.)
2. Cut the tripe into 2-inch slices; set aside.
3. In a mortar, pound to a paste the garlic and green hot pepper; set aside.
4. Heat oil in a top-of-range casserole. Sauté onion, then add tripe, ham, tomato, rum, seasoning paste, thyme, and bay leaves. Simmer 20 minutes. Serve immediately.

6 to 8 servings

Martinique Stuffed Chicken in Rum

1 roaster chicken (about 4 pounds)
1 lime, halved
  Salt and pepper
2 white bread slices with crusts
    trimmed
1 cup milk
1 package (3 ounces) cream cheese
2 tablespoons amber rum
½ cup chopped chicken livers
2 pork sausage links, casing removed
    and meat chopped finely
1 scallion or green onion, chopped
1 tablespoon chopped parsley
⅛ teaspoon cayenne or red pepper
  Salt and pepper (optional)

1. Rub chicken skin with the cut side of lime. Season with salt and pepper. Remove the fat deposits from the opening of the cavity. Set chicken and fat aside.
2. Soak bread in milk. Set aside.
3. Combine cream cheese, rum, chicken liver, sausage, scallion, parsley, and cayenne.
4. Squeeze bread and add to mixture; discard milk. Add salt and pepper, if desired. Mix well.
5. Stuff cavity of chicken with the mixture, then tie chicken legs and wings to hold close to body.
6. Place chicken, breast side up, on rack in a shallow roasting pan. Lay reserved fat across breast.
7. Roast in a 375°F oven about 2 hours.
8. Garnish with **watercress** and serve with Smothered Mixed Vegetables (page 57).

4 to 6 servings

Braised Chicken and Onions
(Maman Poule à la Chaudière)

1 stewing chicken (about 4 pounds)
  Papaya leaves
1 lime, halved
1 orange, halved
  Salt and freshly ground pepper
    to taste
3 tablespoons soybean, olive, or
    peanut oil
3 tablespoons bacon drippings
2 tablespoons water
24 small onions
2 cups chicken stock
2 tablespoons butter
2 tablespoons cornstarch
  Chopped parsley
  Chopped scallions or green onions

1. Truss chicken. Wrap in papaya leaves and refrigerate for 12 hours.
2. Rub the chicken with the cut sides of the lime and orange. Season with salt and pepper.
3. Heat oil and bacon drippings in a Dutch oven. Brown chicken. Add water and cover.
4. Cook in a 375°F oven about 2 hours, or until almost tender; turn occasionally and stir the juices. Add stock if more liquid is needed.
5. Add onions and continue cooking until onions are tender and well browned (about 30 minutes).
6. Place chicken and onions on a large serving platter. Carve bird.
7. Pour stock into Dutch oven and set over medium heat to deglaze. Mix butter and cornstarch and add to stock. Stir until sauce is slightly thicker.
8. Pour sauce over meat and sprinkle with chopped parsley and scallions. Serve with Coconut and Rice (page 59).

6 to 8 servings

Barbecued Chicken, Quail, or Guinea Fowl

Chicken, quail, or guinea fowl
Creole Barbecue Sauce (page 63)

1. Split the birds in half and remove the backbone and neck.
2. Marinate birds overnight in Creole Barbecue Sauce.
3. Place bird halves on a grill 5 inches from glowing coals. Barbecue 25 minutes, turning several times and basting with the barbecue sauce.
4. Serve with **barbecued yams** (see Yams and Sweet Potatoes, page 58).

Allow ½ bird per serving

Chicken with Cashews

In the Caribbean, this dish is traditionally served with preserves made from the cashew fruit, but in the United States, guava jelly is an acceptable substitute.

2 broiler-fryer chickens (about
    2 pounds each), cut in pieces
1 lime, halved
    Salt, freshly ground pepper, and
      cayenne or red pepper
½ cup peanut oil
4 shallots, minced
¾ cup dry white wine
½ cup chicken broth
1 cup split cashews
½ cup amber rum
2 tablespoons butter
2 tablespoons cornstarch

1. Rub chicken with the cut side of lime. Season with salt, pepper, and cayenne.
2. Heat oil in a Dutch oven and sauté the chicken until golden brown. Add shallots and brown. Add wine and chicken broth. Cover. Simmer over low heat 25 minutes. Add cashews and simmer about 10 minutes.
3. Remove chicken and cashews with a slotted spoon and keep warm. Remove excess fat from Dutch oven, leaving drippings. Deglaze with rum.
4. Mix butter and cornstarch and add to drippings. Cook over high heat, stirring constantly, until sauce is slightly thicker.
5. Pour sauce over chicken and nuts. Serve with Bananas à l'Antillaise and Guava Jelly (page 53).

6 servings

Chicken with Peas *(Poulet Pois France)*

3 broiler-fryer chickens
    (3 pounds each), cut in pieces
1 tablespoon lime juice
    Salt and freshly ground pepper
¼ cup soybean oil
1 shallot
1 garlic clove
1 teaspoon dried thyme
1 green hot pepper or
    3 dried Italian pepper pods
2 cups chicken stock
3 pounds fresh green peas, shelled
2 tablespoons butter
2 tablespoons cornstarch

1. Season chicken with lime juice, salt, and pepper.
2. Heat oil in a Dutch oven and sauté the chicken pieces until golden brown on all sides.
3. In a mortar, pound to a paste the shallot and garlic. Add seasoning paste, thyme, green hot pepper, 1 cup stock, and peas to the chicken. Reduce heat and simmer 25 minutes, or until chicken and peas are tender.
4. Remove chicken, peas, and hot pepper to a heated platter and keep hot. Add remaining stock to Dutch oven; bring to a boil. Mix butter and cornstarch and add to stock. Stir until sauce is slightly thicker. Add salt and pepper, if desired.
5. Garnish chicken with **chopped parsley** and serve sauce in a sauceboat.

About 10 servings

Squab with Peas: Follow recipe for Chicken with Peas, allowing ½ **squab per serving.** Carve birds and place meat on slices of **bread fried in butter.** Pour sauce over meat and croutons.

Quail with Peas: Follow recipe for Chicken with Peas, substituting **1 cup red wine** for the cooking stock. Allow **1 quail per serving.** Carve birds and place meat on slices of **bread fried in butter.** Pour sauce over meat and croutons.

Roast Turkey

1 ready-to-cook turkey
   (reserve giblets)
1 lime, halved
1 orange, halved
1 teaspoon monosodium glutamate
   Salt and freshly ground pepper
¼ cup olive oil
1 tablespoon tomato paste
1 garlic clove, crushed in a
   garlic press
1 quart water
1 large onion, sliced
4 parsley sprigs
1 bay leaf
2 teaspoons salt
   Lettuce
   Cherry tomato
   Avocado half
   Green pepper ring
2 tablespoons butter
2 tablespoons cornstarch

1. Rub the skin of the bird with the cut side of the lime and orange. Sprinkle monosodium glutamate, salt, and pepper over surface. Refrigerate 2 hours.
2. Combine oil, tomato paste, and garlic. Brush mixture over bird. Set on a rack in a shallow roasting pan.
3. Roast, uncovered, in a 375°F oven until turkey tests done (the thickest part of the drumstick feels soft when pressed with fingers, or meat thermometer inserted in the thickest part of inner thigh muscle registers 180° to 185°F).
4. Meanwhile, prepare giblet broth. Put turkey neck and giblets (except liver), water, onion, parsley, bay leaf, and salt in a saucepan. Cover and simmer about 2 hours, or until giblets are tender. Add the liver the last 15 minutes of cooking. Strain.
5. Carve turkey and arrange meat on a bed of lettuce. Garnish with tomato, avocado, and green pepper.
6. Remove excess fat from roasting pan. Pour in 2 cups giblet broth to deglaze over medium heat.
7. Mix butter and cornstarch and add to broth. Stir until sauce is slightly thicker.
8. Serve sauce with turkey.

Turkey Croquettes

2 tablespoons butter
2 tablespoons minced shallot
1½ tablespoons flour
½ cup chicken broth
2 egg yolks, beaten
2 cups ground turkey
1 tablespoon chopped parsley
1 teaspoon salt
¼ teaspoon freshly ground pepper
2 egg yolks
2 teaspoons cooking oil
   Dry bread crumbs
   Fat for deep frying,
      heated to 375°F

1. Melt butter in a skillet. Cook shallot over low heat until translucent. Stir in flour. Gradually add chicken broth, blending until smooth.
2. Remove from heat and beat in 2 egg yolks. Add turkey, parsley, salt, and pepper; mix well.
3. Spread mixture on a platter and cool in refrigerator.
4. Shape mixture into small balls. Coat balls with a mixture of 2 egg yolks and oil and then roll in bread crumbs.
5. Fry in heated fat until golden. Drain on absorbent paper.
6. Serve with Tomato Sauce Creole (page 63).

Roast Rabbit Guadeloupe

1 ready-to-cook rabbit (about 4 pounds); reserve the giblets
1 cup wine vinegar
2 garlic cloves, crushed in a garlic press
1 teaspoon salt
¼ teaspoon freshly ground pepper
⅛ teaspoon cayenne or red pepper
⅛ teaspoon ground cloves
1 package (7 ounces) stuffing mix
3 tablespoons butter, melted
1 tablespoon chopped onion
1 tablespoon chopped chives
1 tablespoon chopped parsley
2 basil leaves, chopped
⅛ teaspoon dried thyme
⅛ teaspoon cayenne or red pepper
2 tablespoons olive oil
1 tablespoon lime juice

1. Marinate rabbit in a mixture of wine vinegar, garlic, salt, pepper, ⅛ teaspoon cayenne, and cloves for 2 hours.
2. Prepare stuffing mix according to package directions. Add butter, onion, chives, parsley, basil, thyme, and ⅛ teaspoon cayenne. Chop the rabbit giblets and add to the stuffing mixture.
3. Spoon stuffing into rabbit. Using skewers, close the body cavity.
4. Brush the skin of the rabbit with a mixture of oil and lime juice.
5. Roast in a 425°F oven 45 minutes, or until tender and well browned.
6. Serve with Caribbean Rice or French-Fried Breadfruit (pages 59, 52).

4 to 6 servings

Duck Bigarade

A bigarade is a small, bitter orange which grows in profusion in the islands. The sour orange taste can be duplicated by mixing lime and orange juices.

2 limes, halved
1 ready-to-cook duck (about 5 pounds)
Salt, freshly ground pepper, and cayenne or red pepper
2 cups firmly packed brown sugar
1 cup water
2 teaspoons vanilla extract
½ cup orange peel strips
4 small oranges, halved and seeded
2 cups chicken broth
¼ cup orange juice
½ cup amber rum
¼ cup butter
¼ cup cornstarch

1. Squeeze lime juice over the entire duck. Season with salt, pepper, and cayenne. Place on a rack in a roasting pan.
2. Roast uncovered in a 425°F oven 25 minutes. Turn oven control to 350°F and continue to roast 30 minutes.
3. Combine brown sugar, water, and vanilla extract in a large, heavy saucepan. Bring to a boil over high heat and boil about 6 minutes. Add orange peel and orange halves and continue boiling 1 minute. Remove from heat and cool. Set ¼ cup syrup aside in a small saucepan.
4. Transfer duck to a warm platter. Remove fat from roasting pan. Stir in chicken broth and orange juice to deglaze. Heat the rum, ignite it, and when flames die down, pour it into the chicken broth.
5. Heat the reserved syrup until it caramelizes. Add to chicken broth mixture and blend well.
6. Mix butter and cornstarch and add to roasting pan. Cook over medium heat, stirring constantly, until the gravy is slightly thicker.
7. Carve the duck. Sprinkle the glazed orange peel strips over the meat. Pour a little gravy over the meat. Serve remaining gravy separately. Arrange glazed orange halves around the duck, alternating with bouquets of **watercress**. Serve with Caribbean Rice (page 59).

4 servings

Wild Duck Pâté

2 wild ducks (about 4 pounds each);
  reserve livers
¼ cup olive oil
  Juice of 2 limes
1 garlic clove, halved
  Water
1 carrot
1 leek
1 teaspoon salt
⅛ teaspoon pepper
1 cup port wine
2 bay leaves
1 small onion, minced
1 green hot pepper
⅛ teaspoon thyme
3 tablespoons olive oil
3 tablespoons butter
½ pound beef liver, cubed
¼ cup amber rum
1 egg
  Lard
  Truffles (optional)
  Bay leaves and green hot peppers
    for garnish

1. Marinate the ducks for ½ hour in a mixture of ¼ cup oil and lime juice. Rub ducks with the cut surface of garlic clove.
2. Place birds in a Dutch oven and cover with water; add carrot, leek, salt, and pepper and bring to a boil. Simmer covered over low heat until birds are tender.
3. Remove birds from broth and cool. Reserve ¼ cup broth; store remaining broth for future use. Remove the meat from the carcasses, cutting the breast meat into long, even strips.
4. Mix port wine, bay leaves, onion, pepper, and thyme; marinate the breast meat for ½ hour. Set aside remaining duck meat.
5. Heat 3 tablespoons oil and butter in a medium skillet. Sauté duck livers and beef liver over high heat until golden. Warm the rum, ignite it, and pour it, still flaming, over the livers. Stir in ¼ cup of the reserved broth to deglaze the skillet.
6. Purée in an electric blender the liver mixture, reserved duck meat, and egg.
7. Coat heavily with lard 1 large terrine or loaf dish, or 2 small terrines or loaf dishes. Put in half the puréed mixture, then arrange the marinated strips of duck breast on top with slices of truffles, if desired. Cover with the remaining duck mixture, then with a thick coat of lard.
8. Garnish with bay leaves and green hot peppers. Cover terrine and place in a pan of hot water.
9. Bake at 375°F about 1½ hours.
10. Wipe clean the sides of the terrine. Cool and store covered in refrigerator up to a week.
11. To serve, remove bay leaves and peppers; slice pâté and accompany with salad.

Curried Duck Martinique
(Colombo de Canard Martiniquaise)

3 cups coarsely chopped
  cooked duck
3 cups sliced mushrooms
6 tablespoons butter, melted
1 cup diced apple
⅓ cup grated onion
1 garlic clove, crushed in a
    garlic press
3 tablespoons flour
1 tablespoon curry powder
½ teaspoon salt
¼ teaspoon freshly ground pepper
1 cup whipping cream
½ cup duck stock
    (made from cooking the carcass)
3 tablespoons Madeira or
    sweet sherry

1. Cook duck and mushrooms in half the melted butter in a skillet over low heat, until the duck is slightly browned and the mushrooms are tender. Remove from heat and cover.
2. Sauté apple, onion, and garlic in remaining butter in a large skillet until soft. Remove skillet from the heat and stir in flour, curry, salt, and pepper.
3. Place skillet over low heat and blend in cream, stock, and Madeira. Stir constantly until the mixture thickens. Stir in the duck and mushroom mixture.
4. Serve with **cooked white rice** tossed with **1 cup diced banana.**

6 servings

Pot-Roasted Wild Duck

4 wild ducks (about 2 pounds each)
 Amber rum
8 limes, peeled
8 peppercorns, cracked
 Papaya leaves
 Bacon drippings
3 tablespoons soybean oil
12 shallots
⅓ cup amber rum
½ cup stock
1 carrot
1 garlic clove, crushed in a
    garlic press
1 thyme sprig
1 parsley sprig
1 green hot pepper
2 cups hot stock
2 tablespoons butter
2 tablespoons cornstarch
 Salt and pepper to taste
8 slices bread, toasted
¼ cup butter

1. Wipe the duck with rum. Place 2 limes and 2 peppercorns in the cavity of each duck. Wrap the birds in papaya leaves to tenderize and refrigerate 12 hours.
2. Brush bacon drippings on each bird. Heat the oil in a Dutch oven and sauté ducks and shallots until the birds are brown on all sides.
3. Heat rum, ignite it, and pour it, while still flaming, over the birds. Add the ½ cup stock, carrot, garlic, thyme, parsley, and hot pepper. Cover Dutch oven.
4. Cook in a 475°F oven 30 minutes.
5. Cut the breasts in one piece and slice off remaining meat; reserve. Discard limes and peppercorns.
6. In a mortar, pound the carcasses until broken up. Pour the hot stock into the Dutch oven; add the broken carcasses and boil 10 minutes. Remove the hot pepper. Strain the stock and return to the Dutch oven.
7. Mix butter and cornstarch. Add to the stock; stir over medium heat until slightly thickened. Add salt and pepper to taste.
8. Fry toasted bread in butter until golden and crisp. Arrange meat on croutons. Pour sauce over all.
9. Garnish with Stuffed Sweet Peppers (page 58). Serve remaining sauce from a sauceboat.

8 servings

Guinea Stew

½ teaspoon monosodium glutamate
 Salt and freshly ground pepper
1 guinea fowl (2½ to 3 pounds)
1 lime, halved
¼ pound salt pork, cubed
4 parsley sprigs
2 scallions or green onions, chopped
2 garlic cloves
2 cloves
½ teaspoon salt
¼ cup soybean oil
½ cup amber rum
2 cups red wine
1 cup chicken stock
12 shallots
2 carrots, sliced
2 turnips, sliced
1 tablespoon butter
1 tablespoon cornstarch

1. Sprinkle monosodium glutamate, salt, and pepper over bird and refrigerate overnight. The next day, rub the skin with the cut side of the lime. Cut bird into pieces.
2. Render salt pork over medium heat in a Dutch oven. When crisp, remove the cracklings.
3. In a mortar, pound to a paste the parsley, scallions, garlic, cloves, and salt. Add the seasoning paste and oil to the Dutch oven.
4. Sauté the meat until golden brown on all sides.
5. Heat rum, ignite it, and pour it, still flaming, over the meat. Add wine and stock; reduce heat, cover, and simmer 30 mintues.
6. Add shallots, carrots, and turnips. Simmer until meat and vegetables are tender.
7. Place meat and vegetables on a serving platter.
8. Mix butter and cornstarch; add to liquid in Dutch oven and stir over high heat until sauce is slightly thickened. Season with salt and pepper, if necessary. Pour sauce over meat and vegetables.
9. Serve with Caribbean Rice (pages 59).

2 servings

Chicken Stew: Follow recipe for Guinea Stew, substituting **1 broiler-fryer chicken (about 2 pounds)** for guinea fowl.

Barbecued Wild Game Birds

4 ready-to-cook wild game birds such as duckling, snipe, teal, or woodcock
Amber rum
6 peppercorns
4 parsley sprigs
3 garlic cloves
1 green hot pepper
1 tablespoon salt
1 tablespoon olive or peanut oil
1 cup red wine
Bacon drippings
Dry bread crumbs
Creole Barbecue Sauce (page 63)

1. Brush surface of birds with rum. Split birds in half and pound with a meat hammer.
2. In a mortar, pound to a paste the peppercorns, parsley, garlic, pepper, and salt. Mix seasoning paste with olive oil and wine. Pour marinade over birds and refrigerate 12 hours.
3. Thoroughly drain bird halves. Brush with bacon drippings and coat with bread crumbs.
4. Barbecue bird halves in a hinged grill 4 inches from glowing coals about 10 minutes on each side, basting twice with Creole Barbecue Sauce; time depends on their size. Turn birds once and baste again.
5. Birds should be eaten on the rare side; when birds are pricked with a fork, a droplet of blood should surface slowly.
6. Serve with Purée of Breadfruit (page 52).

Teal on the Spit

Teal, a small wild duck, is in season October to February.

4 teals; reserve livers
1 orange, halved
8 chicken livers
1 tablespoon flour
¼ teaspoon garlic powder
Salt and pepper
2 tablespoons olive oil
4 bacon slices
2 tablespoons flour
2 tablespoons butter
1 can (13 ounces) clear consommé madrilène
1½ teaspoons lime juice
1½ teaspoons orange juice

1. Rub teals with cut sides of orange halves. Set aside.
2. Coat the teal livers and chicken livers with a mixture of 1 tablespoon flour, garlic powder, salt, and pepper. Heat oil and sauté the livers until golden brown.
3. Put the livers into the bird cavities. Wrap each bird in a slice of bacon, securing with skewers.
4. Spear birds on a spit and broil on the electric broiler about 25 minutes or, if charcoal is used, place the spitted bird 4 inches from the hot coals and turn often.
5. Brown 2 tablespoons flour in butter in a small saucepan over high heat. Add enough consommé madrilène to just moisten the mixture, stirring rapidly with a whisk. While it thickens, slowly pour in the remaining consommé in a thin stream. Boil rapidly, uncovered, stirring constantly for about 4 minutes, or until the sauce is reduced to ½ cup. Remove from heat and add lime juice and orange juice.
6. Serve teal with Tomatoes Stuffed with Rice and Peanuts (page 57) and the sauce separately.

4 servings

Ortolans on Croutons

8 ortolans
½ lime
Salt and freshly ground pepper
½ cup cubed salt pork
¼ cup amber rum
½ cup red wine
1 tablespoon butter
1 tablespoon cornstarch
8 white bread slices with crusts trimmed
¼ cup butter

1. Truss ortolans. Rub the skin with the cut side of the lime half. Season with salt and pepper.
2. Render the salt pork over high heat in a Dutch oven. Sauté ortolans for 6 minutes, or until well browned.
3. Heat rum, ignite it, and pour it, still flaming, over the birds. Place birds on a serving platter.
4. Pour wine into Dutch oven to deglaze. Mix 1 tablespoon butter and cornstarch and add to wine. Stir until sauce is slightly thicker.
5. Make croutons by frying bread slices in butter until brown on both sides.
6. Serve each ortolan on a crouton, top with a slice of sautéed liver pâté, if desired, and pour sauce over all.

8 servings

FRUITS, VEGETABLES, CEREALS, AND BREADS

Guadeloupe and Martinique import all but their tropical fruits, root vegetables, and tropical leaf vegetables from France, Haiti, because of her geography of mountains and plains, is blessed with crops of both the temperate and tropical zones. The vegetables are picked and sped to market, so that less than twelve hours elapse between the field and the kitchen.

For the peasant woman, a trip to market is an occasion not to be missed despite the weight of the basket on her head. It is an opportunity to gossip, to see the town, to buy a trinket. The money she makes is her own, and her man will not take it from her. When she walks back, her basket will be heavy with the wares of exchange. Because cash is hard to come by and has to be bought with extra labor in a barter economy, it both delights and breaks a woman's heart to buy. Therefore she will, before leaving the market, go from stall to stall, extend the bargaining and haggling time as long as she can, almost lose her head in anger and anxiety over being "had" by the city *marchande*. The latter will play her like a fish. Secure in the covetousness she sees in her client's eyes, she will shrewdly push her through the gamut of emotions, will wring next to the last penny from her, and when the countrywoman despairs, she will, because she understands need, throw in a bonus, a *degui*, which will change the frown of anger to smiles of gratification.

A good city cook shops for fresh produce every day. In Haiti can be found small potatoes, cauliflower, baby carrots, wild strawberries and blackberries, peas which are a little more mealy than the varieties we know, innumerable varieties of beans, peppers both sweet and pungent, melons, watermelons, and pumpkin. There are cucumbers and squashes and chayotes, onions, lettuce, and, grouped together under the name of *vivres alimentaires*, breadfruit, plantains of many kind, bananas, malanga, several kinds of sweet potatoes and yams. These latter are often boiled all together for the evening meal with some of the cooking liquid, coarse salt, and hot peppers and pounded into a paste in a huge mortar. This is the *Tom-tom* of slavery days.

Several varieties of millet, maize, and rice are also offered, as well as a wide variety of exotic fruit such as mangoes, papayas, avocados, soursop.

"Confitures" stems from "comfits," or preserves. The fruits from which they are made are varied and plentiful in the islands.

Breads play a minor role in Caribbean meals; emphasis is placed instead on fresh fruits and vegetables. Corn bread is popular since it balances the spiciness of other foods, and Biscuits Port-au-Prince offer a nice change from the traditional baking powder biscuit.

There is a section in the produce market where, especially on Saturday mornings, herbs can be found such as mint, fennel, rosemary, basil, bay leaf, vanilla pods in bundles, and along with Palma Christi, many other leaves for healing, bathing, or for repelling insects and bad spirits. Garlic, however, has to be imported.

Purée of Breadfruit

1 breadfruit (1½ pounds),
   peeled and cubed
1 cup whipping cream
   Salt, freshly ground pepper, and
   cayenne or red pepper to taste

1. Cook breadfruit in lightly salted water until tender; drain.
2. Process breadfruit, a small amount at a time, with a small amount of cream, in an electric blender to make a purée. Mix in seasonings.

Note: If desired, force breadfruit through a food mill and beat in cream, slightly whipped, and the seasonings.

French-Fried Breadfruit

1 large heavy breadfruit
   Oil for deep frying,
   heated to 365°F
   Salt to taste

1. Cut the breadfruit into wedges about 1½ inches thick; discard the center. Soak the wedges in lightly salted water 30 minutes. Dry with absorbent paper.
2. Fry breadfruit wedges, a few at a time, in heated oil until golden (about 8 minutes). Drain on absorbent paper. Salt lightly and serve very hot where you would serve French-fried potatoes.

Bananas à l'Antillaise (Bananes-Figues au Vin Blanc)

6 **green-tipped bananas,
    peeled and halved**
2 **cups dry white wine**
Salt to taste
2 **tablespoons butter**
2 **tablespoons flour**
⅛ **teaspoon mace**
⅛ **teaspoon cloves**
Cayenne or red pepper to taste

1. Put bananas into a saucepan with wine and salt. Bring to a boil, cover, and simmer 25 minutes.
2. Blend butter, flour, mace, cloves, and pepper.
3. Remove fruit from saucepan. Stir butter mixture into liquid in saucepan. Boil and stir 3 minutes.
4. Serve the fruit and sauce in a dish as an accompaniment to roast pork.

Boiled Plantain

Green plantain
½ **lime**
Boiling salted water

1. Remove the skin and scrape the threads from plantain. Rub the fruit with the cut side of a lime.
2. Cook in boiling salted water 30 minutes.

Grated Green Papaya Salad Guadeloupe

1 **hard green papaya (1 pound),
    pared and grated**
Oil-and-vinegar French dressing
½ **cup raisins, plumped in
    boiling water**

Season grated papaya with French dressing and garnish with raisins.

Guava Preserves

5 **cups peeled ripe guava slices**
Sugar
Limes, halved

1. Put guava slices into a deep pot and cover with water; bring to a boil, reduce heat, and simmer until fruit is tender.
2. Measure fruit and add an equal amount of sugar.
3. For 4 cups of fruit, use 2 limes. Discard center and core from lime halves and squeeze. Add the juice and shells to the fruit and sugar. Cook at a rolling boil 10 minutes. Skim.
4. Pack hot mixture into sterilized jars, seal, and store.

Guava Jelly: Follow recipe for Guava Preserves for cooking guava. Allow to drip through a jelly bag or through a strainer lined with cheesecloth. For a clear jelly, do not squeeze the bag. Measure juice and add an equal amount of sugar and 1 tablespoon lime juice per cup of liquid. Boil at a rolling boil until mixture sheets from side of spoon. Skim and cool. Pack in sterilized jars, seal, and store.

Lime Marmalade

5 pounds limes
5 quarts water
10 pounds sugar

1. Rinse limes. Slice them thinly and put into a deep kettle along with water. Cover; bring to a boil, reduce heat, and cook slowly 15 minutes. Add sugar; cook uncovered until syrup sheets off the side of a spoon.
2. Pack into sterilized jars, seal, and store.

Lime Preserves Niniche Gaillard

4 dozen small limes
5 pounds rock salt
Sugar

1. Put limes into a jelly bag or old pillowcase with rock salt. Rub limes against rock salt for 2 minutes with a rolling motion. Remove limes from bag and wash each one to remove salt.
2. Put the limes into a kettle with water to cover, bring to a boil, and discard water. Repeat this procedure 6 times to soften the limes. Remove as many seeds as you can from the limes, using a crochet hook. Rinse under running cold water.
3. Weigh limes, put into kettle, and add an equal weight of sugar and 1 cup water per pound of fruit. Bring to a boil over high heat and cook at a rolling boil until syrup sheets off side of a spoon.
4. Pour into sterilized jars, seal, and store.

Mango Preserves

16 small limes, peeled and
    cut in small pieces
8 pounds firm-ripe mango chips
½ cup grated fresh ginger root
4 pounds sugar

1. Put all ingredients into a kettle; stir. Bring to a boil, reduce heat, and simmer until mango is soft and juice is reduced by half its volume. Skim.
2. Pack mixture into sterilized jars, seal, and store.

Tamarind Marmalade

1 quart shelled tamarind nuts or
    seeds
Sugar

1. Boil tamarind nuts in a large amount of water until soft.
2. Sieve the nuts to remove fiber and seeds. Measure the pulp and mix it with an equal amount of sugar in a saucepan. Bring to a boil over high heat, then reduce heat and simmer, stirring constantly, until the mixture coats a spoon.
3. Pack into sterilized jars, seal, and store.

Kenscoff Strawberry Preserves

4 cups wild strawberries, washed,
    drained, and hulled
6 cups sugar
¾ cup lime juice

1. Put strawberries into a large kettle and add sugar. Cover kettle with a piece of glass and set kettle in a sunny place for 3 hours.
2. Set kettle over low heat and bring to a boil; boil 8 minutes, stirring constantly. Add lime juice and boil 3 minutes.
3. Cool mixture, then skim and stir. Pack into sterilized jars, seal, and store.

Artichokes à la Four Thieves

8 artichokes
Boiling salted water
Four Thieves Sauce (page 62)

1. Wash artichokes under running water. Let them stand 10 minutes in cold salted water; drain.
2. With a sharp kitchen knife, remove stem and bottom leaves from each artichoke, and with kitchen shears snip ¼ inch off the top of each leaf.
3. Cook the artichokes uncovered in a pot of boiling salted water 30 minutes; drain and cool.
4. To serve, gently spread artichoke leaves to the sides and, with a grapefruit knife, remove the very small purplish leaves and the choke that covers the bottom, scraping it clean. Accompany with hot Four Thieves Sauce.

8 servings

Braised Lettuce

8 small heads Boston lettuce or
   16 heads Bibb lettuce
1 cup chicken broth
   Juice of 1 lime
6 tablespoons butter
   Salt and freshly ground pepper
      to taste

1. Rinse lettuce under running cold water; tie each head firmly with string.
2. Put lettuce into a skillet with broth, lime juice, butter, salt, and pepper. Bring to a boil, then cover, reduce heat, and simmer 15 minutes.
3. Remove cover, increase heat, and boil rapidly until no liquid remains and edges of lettuce are golden. Remove the string. Serve with roasts.

Barbecued Sweet Peppers

4 red sweet peppers
4 green sweet peppers
   Peanut oil
   French dressing

1. Core the peppers and cut each into three strips.
2. Coat both sides of pepper strips with oil; let them stand 40 minutes.
3. Brush pepper strips lightly with oil and place in a hinged grill. Barbecue 2 inches from ash-covered coals, allowing peppers to blister.
4. Chill and serve with French dressing as an antipasto or with other marinated vegetables.

Cooked Hearts of Palm

To obtain this vegetable a full-grown palm tree has to be felled. It is, therefore, understandable that heart of palm is expensive. It looks like a chunk of ivory and is rarely found in the market stalls.

½ cup cubed salt pork
2 cups cubed heart of palm
1 cup chicken broth

1. Render salt pork in a Dutch oven. Add heart of palm and broth; simmer covered over medium heat until no liquid remains and heart of palm is tender.
2. Serve hot with Béchamel Sauce (page 62) or cold with **French dressing.**

Raw Heart of Palm Salad

1 pound heart of palm
Mayonnaise or French dressing

1. Slice the heart of palm paper thin. Soak it 1 hour in cold water. Drain well on absorbent paper.
2. Serve heart of palm with mayonnaise or in a tossed green salad with French dressing.

Smothered Cabbage (Chou Touffe)

2 small heads cabbage
2 tablespoons peanut oil
1 onion, minced
1 garlic clove, crushed in a garlic press
8 bacon slices
½ cup stock
Freshly ground pepper to taste
3 drops Tabasco
1 tablespoon butter
1 tablespoon cornstarch
1 teaspoon tomato paste
1 teaspoon lime juice
Lime wedges

1. Remove wilted leaves from cabbage. Quarter and core cabbage.
2. Heat oil in a top-of-range casserole, add onion and garlic and sauté until golden. Add cabbage pieces and lay a bacon slice on each. Add stock, pepper, and Tabasco. Bring to a boil, reduce heat, and simmer covered 15 minutes; cabbage will still be a little crisp.
3. Meanwhile, mix butter and cornstarch.
4. Transfer cabbage to a heated platter. Mix tomato paste and lime juice into cooking liquid and bring rapidly to a boil, then add butter-cornstarch mixture and stir until liquid is slightly thicker.
5. To serve, pour sauce over cabbage. Accompany with lime wedges.

8 servings

Fried Okra Pods

2 pounds large okra pods, washed and stems trimmed
Salt, pepper, and cayenne or red pepper to taste
1 egg yolk
1 tablespoon olive oil
1 cup dried bread crumbs
Oil for deep frying, heated to 365°F
Watercress and wedges of avocado and tomato for garnish

1. Cook okra in lightly salted boiling water 7 minutes. Drain and season.
2. Roll them in egg yolk beaten with oil, then in bread crumbs.
3. Fry the pods in heated oil until golden and drain on absorbent paper.
4. Serve surrounded with watercress, avocado, and tomato.

Sweet Potato Soufflé

2 cups hot mashed sweet potatoes
⅓ cup hot milk
⅓ cup amber rum
¼ cup butter
⅛ teaspoon nutmeg
Dash Tabasco
1 teaspoon grated lime peel
4 egg yolks, beaten
5 egg whites, stiffly beaten

1. Beat sweet potatoes, milk, rum, and butter together until smooth. Add nutmeg, Tabasco, lime peel, and beaten egg yolk; beat well. Fold in beaten egg white.
2. Pour into a well-greased 1½-quart soufflé dish. Set in pan of hot water.
3. Bake at 425°F 25 to 30 minutes. Serve at once.

Ratatouille of Pumpkin

1 cup diced salt pork
4 slices ham or Canadian bacon
3 scallions or green onions including
    green tops, cut in pieces
3 garlic cloves
5 parsley sprigs
6 dried Italian pepper pods or
    ½ green hot pepper
2½ pounds pumpkin meat,
    pared and cubed
2 cups stock or chicken broth
3 tablespoons butter
¼ cup chopped parsley

1. Sauté salt pork and ham in a Dutch oven until brown.
2. In a mortar, pound together to a paste the scallions, garlic,
parsley, and pepper pods.
3. Add pumpkin, seasoning paste, and stock to Dutch oven.
Cover and simmer until pumpkin is tender enough to mash
with a fork.
4. Remove cover and, stirring constantly, cook off most of the
liquid, being careful that pumpkin does not stick. Add butter
and stir until melted.
5. Serve sprinkled with parsley.

Smothered Mixed Vegetables *(Touffé)*

8 small carrots, sliced
8 small potatoes
4 medium white turnips, pared
    and sliced
4 medium tomatoes, peeled, seeded,
    and quartered
2 small chayote or zucchini, sliced
1 green and 1 red sweet pepper,
    cut in strips
1 small eggplant (unpeeled), diced
    Cauliflower chunks
½ cup green peas
½ cup lima beans
2 tablespoons peanut oil
1 large Spanish onion, sliced
1 cup stock or beef broth
¼ cup peanut oil
1 tablespoon salt
    Freshly ground pepper
1 garlic clove, crushed in a
    garlic press
4 dried Italian pepper pods or
    1 pink hot pepper
1 tablespoon tomato paste

1. Arrange in a top-of-range casserole with lid the sliced carrot, potatoes, turnip slices, tomato quarters, sliced chayote,
pepper strips, diced eggplant, cauliflower chunks, peas, and
beans.
2. Heat 2 tablespoons oil in a skillet over medium heat. Add
onion and sauté until golden. Add stock, ¼ cup oil, salt, pepper, and garlic; pour over vegetables in casserole. Lay pepper
pods over vegetables; cover and cook covered over low heat 45
minutes.
3. Remove cover, increase heat, and cook off most of the liquid. Remove peppers and stir tomato paste into vegetable mixture. Serve with **pepper steak** or well-browned **spareribs** or
pork chops.

Tomatoes Stuffed with Rice and Peanuts

8 medium tomatoes
    Caribbean Rice (page 59;
      ¾ recipe)
½ cup coarsely chopped peanuts
¾ cup grated Parmesan cheese
2 cups Tomato Sauce Creole
    (page 63)

1. Hollow out tomatoes, reserving pulp to make tomato sauce.
Invert tomato shells to drain.
2. Prepare rice and mix in peanuts and ½ cup cheese.
3. Stuff tomato shells with rice mixture. Sprinkle remaining
cheese over top. Arrange in a baking dish.
4. Bake at 375°F 20 minutes. Spoon hot tomato sauce around
the tomatoes.

Chayotes Martinique
(Christophines à la Martiniquaise)

4 chayotes
3 tablespoons butter
Salt, pepper, and cayenne or
  red pepper to taste
1 teaspoon ground ginger or grated
  fresh ginger
2 cups chicken stock or bouillon
1 beef marrow bone

1. Wash chayotes, cut into halves, and remove seeds. Coat the insides with butter and season with salt, pepper, cayenne, and ginger. Place chayotes in a baking dish and pour stock into dish.
2. Bake at 350°F 30 minutes.
3. Meanwhile, cook marrow bone in boiling salted water 20 minutes. Remove marrow and cut into 8 slices.
4. Garnish each chayote half with a marrow slice and grind a little black pepper over each.

8 servings

Yams and Sweet Potatoes

Yams or sweet potatoes
Salt
Butter (optional)

Boil yams and serve plain sprinkled with salt and, if desired, topped with butter. Or barbecue yams on a grill 4 inches from ash-covered coals, turning frequently, until soft. Or bake yams until tender.

Stuffed Chayotes

4 large chayotes, halved
3 tablespoons peanut oil
1 tablespoon minced onion
3 drops Tabasco
Freshly ground pepper to taste
1 cup cooked ground meat
3 tablespoons tomato paste
½ cup grated Parmesan cheese

1. Parboil chayotes in boiling salted water until soft enough to scoop out flesh. Drain. Scoop pulp from skins; reserve skins. Cube pulp.
2. Heat oil in a skillet and mix in onion, Tabasco, and pepper. Add cubed chayote and cooked meat; sauté until chayote is soft. Mash mixture with a fork and blend in tomato paste.
3. Pile mixture into skins and sprinkle with cheese. Brown under a broiler and serve.

8 servings

Stuffed Sweet Peppers

4 red or green sweet peppers,
  halved lengthwise
Stock
1 cup cooked rice
2 cups cooked ground beef, ham,
  or poultry
Shredded cheese
Tomato Sauce Creole (page 63)

1. Parboil pepper halves in stock to cover. Drain peppers and reserve stock.
2. Mix rice and meat; stuff peppers. Sprinkle tops with cheese. Arrange peppers in a baking dish; add reserved stock to dish.
3. Bake at 350°F 30 minutes, or until well browned. Serve in the baking dish and accompany with the sauce.

4 servings

Rice and Beans

2 quarts water
2 cups dried red beans, rinsed
1 can (13¾ ounces) beef broth
Water
1 tablespoon salt
8 parsley sprigs
3 scallions or green onions, chopped
3 garlic cloves
¼ teaspoon dried rosemary
3 tablespoons peanut oil
2 cups rice

1. Bring water to boiling. Add red beans and cook covered for 1½ hours.
2. Drain beans, reserving liquid, and set aside. Add beef broth and enough water to bean liquid to equal 4¾ cups liquid. Set aside.
3. In a mortar, pound together to form a paste the salt, parsley, scallions, garlic, and rosemary.
4. Heat oil and seasoning paste in a Dutch oven over medium heat. Put rice in Dutch oven and stir until well coated with oil. Add reserved liquid and bring to a boil, stirring. Add beans and again bring to a boil. Reduce heat, cover, and cook undisturbed for 20 minutes.
5. Remove cover, stir, and cook about 5 minutes longer, or until no liquid remains.

8 to 10 servings

Caribbean Rice

4 parsley sprigs
3 peppercorns
2 garlic cloves
2 scallions or green onions,
    cut in pieces
1½ teaspoons salt
½ teaspoon thyme
2 tablespoons peanut oil
2 cups rice
4½ cups chicken broth
1 bay leaf
1 green hot pepper or
    ½ teaspoon cayenne or
    red pepper

1. In a mortar, pound parsley, peppercorns, garlic, scallions, salt, and thyme to a paste. Set aside.
2. Heat oil in a large, heavy saucepan; add rice. Stir until all the rice is coated with oil and turns chalky.
3. Add seasoning paste and chicken broth; bring to a boil. Reduce heat and add bay leaf and pepper. Cover saucepan and cook undisturbed for 20 minutes.
4. Remove the cover; continue to cook over low heat for 5 minutes, or until no liquid remains.
5. Discard bay leaf and whole pepper. Fluff rice and serve.

8 servings

Rice and Avocado: Follow recipe for Caribbean Rice. Place **cubed avocado** on top of the rice for the last 5 minutes of cooking. Mix in avocado when rice is fluffed. Serve with Bean Sauce (page 65).

Coconut and Rice: Follow recipe for Caribbean Rice, using **brown rice** and an additional ½ **cup chicken broth**. Add **1 cup freshly grated coconut** along with bay leaf and pepper. Proceed as directed.

Saffron Rice: Steep ½ **teaspoon Spanish saffron** in 2¼ **cups boiling water** until it turns bright orange. Strain. Follow recipe for Caribbean Rice, using saffron water in place of some of the chicken broth to cook the rice.

Cornmeal

1 cup ground cornmeal
3 cups water
4 dried Italian pepper pods or
    1 piece hot pepper
3 garlic cloves
1 parsley sprig
1 tablespoon coarse salt
¼ cup peanut oil
1 medium onion, chopped
¼ cup unsalted butter
    Bean Sauce (page 65)

1. Stir cornmeal into water and let stand 5 minutes.
2. Meanwhile, in a mortar, pound together to a paste the pepper pods, garlic, parsley, and salt.
3. Heat oil in a Dutch oven over medium heat, add onion, and sauté until translucent but not brown. Add the seasoning paste and the cornmeal with water; mix well. Bring to a boil, reduce heat, and simmer covered 30 minutes. Remove cover, add butter, and fluff the cornmeal. Serve with Bean Sauce.

Cornmeal with Beans: Drain **1 large can Puerto Rican red or black beans**, reserving liquid. Add enough **stock** to liquid to make 3 cups. Follow recipe for Cornmeal, substituting bean liquid for water. Add the beans when you fluff the cornmeal.

Cornmeal with Kippers: Follow recipe for Cornmeal. Add desired amount of **flaked canned fillet of kippered herring** when you fluff the cornmeal.

Fried Cornmeal: Follow recipe for Cornmeal or Cornmeal with Beans. Spread 4 cups cornmeal mixture in a rectangular dish; refrigerate overnight. Cut chilled mixture into finger-size strips. Heat **3 tablespoons butter** and **3 tablespoons peanut oil** in a skillet and fry cornmeal over medium heat until golden and crisp.

Corn Bread

1 cup all-purpose flour
1 cup yellow cornmeal
2 teaspoons baking powder
½ teaspoon baking soda
1 teaspoon salt
1 cup milk
2½ teaspoons lime juice
1 egg, beaten
2 tablespoons lard, melted

1. Combine flour, cornmeal, baking powder, baking soda, and salt in a bowl.
2. Mix milk and lime juice; add to dry ingredients along with egg and lard. Mix well, but do not beat. Pour into a greased 11x7x1½-inch baking pan.
3. Bake at 450°F 15 to 20 minutes, or until it is brown and tests done. Cool slightly and cut into squares.

About 8 servings

Biscuits Port-au-Prince

2 cups sifted all-purpose flour
2 teaspoons baking powder
1 teaspoon salt
5 tablespoons vegetable shortening
¾ cup milk

1. Combine flour, baking powder, and salt in a bowl. Cut in shortening with pastry blender or two knives until mixture resembles small peas.
2. Make a well in center of mixture and add milk. Stir with fork until dough holds together.
3. Knead on a lightly floured board 30 seconds. Roll dough to ½-inch thickness. Cut with a floured 1½-inch cutter.
4. Place on greased baking sheets about 1 inch apart.
5. Bake at 425°F 15 to 20 minutes, or until golden brown.

About 2 dozen biscuits

SAUCES AND SALAD DRESSINGS

Juliette

The Caribbean hotels and inns offer a good sampling of elegant French sauces, but these are not the concern of this book. The people of Martinique tend to cook with olive oil, those of the other islands with peanut or soybean oil. Mayonnaise can be bought, but most islanders make their own.

Béchamel Sauce

2 tablespoons butter
3 tablespoons flour
1½ cups hot milk, beef broth, or chicken broth
Salt and pepper to taste
½ cup whipping cream

Melt butter over medium heat; stir in flour. Using a whisk, stir rapidly until smooth. Gradually add milk or other liquid, stirring constantly. Bring sauce to a rapid boil and boil 4 minutes, or until sauce is thick and reduced to half its original volume. Season with salt and pepper. Reduce heat and stir in cream. Heat thoroughly, but do not boil.

About 1⅔ cups

Ti-Malice Sauce

8 large shallots, sliced
Juice of 3 limes
1 cup water
¼ cup bacon drippings
3 garlic cloves
1 fresh green hot pepper or
  2 preserved cherry peppers, centers removed and peppers thinly slivered
⅛ teaspoon ground thyme
5 parsley sprigs

1. Marinate shallots in lime juice 30 minutes, or until they turn pink.
2. Put shallots into a saucepan, add water and bacon drippings, and bring to the boiling point. Set aside.
3. In a mortar, pound together to a paste the garlic, pepper, thyme, and parsley.
4. Add seasoning paste to shallots in saucepan and bring to a boil, stirring to blend.
5. Serve in a sauceboat to accompany fried foods.

Four Thieves Sauce (Sauce des Quatre Voleurs)

2 tablespoons butter
2 tablespoons flour
1½ cups chicken broth
Salt and freshly ground pepper to taste
1 egg yolk
3 tablespoons Four Thieves Vinegar (page 65)
1 egg white, beaten stiff but not dry

1. Melt butter in a saucepan over medium heat. Add flour and, stirring constantly with a whisk, make a lightly browned roux. Continue to stir rapidly with a whisk while gradually adding broth. When all the broth is added, boil 4 minutes to reduce the liquid. Season with salt and pepper.
2. Remove from heat and beat a small amount of hot sauce into egg yolk; return mixture to saucepan. Cool thoroughly.
3. Blend sauce into vinegar. Just before serving, fold in beaten egg white.
4. Serve sauce with cold fish or poultry.

Creole Barbecue Sauce

1 can (28 ounces) Italian plum tomatoes, drained
1 medium onion, finely chopped
⅔ cup olive oil
2 garlic cloves, crushed in a garlic press
¼ cup lime juice
1 teaspoon salt
⅛ teaspoon dried basil
Dash pepper
Bouquet garni
5 drops Tabasco

1. Chop tomatoes; put tomato and onion into a saucepan and cook uncovered over medium heat for 15 minutes.
2. Force tomato mixture through a fine sieve into another saucepan. Discard remaining solids.
3. Add remaining ingredients to saucepan. Stir until blended. Simmer uncovered about 1 hour, stirring occasionally.
4. Brush sauce over meat for barbecuing.

About 3½ cups

Tomato Sauce Creole

⅓ cup peanut oil
2 medium onions, thinly sliced
6 Italian plum tomatoes, peeled, seeded, and finely chopped
½ cup beef stock
Salt and freshly ground pepper to taste
3 drops Tabasco
1 garlic clove, crushed in a garlic press

1. Heat oil in a saucepan, add onion, and cook over low heat until translucent but not browned. Add tomato, stock, and seasonings; stir with a wooden spoon until tomato pulp is cooked to a fine purée.
2. Serve with rice or grilled meats.

Dilled Avocado Sauce for Fish

1 large firm avocado, peeled and cubed
¼ cup olive oil
3 tablespoons lime juice, strained
Salt, pepper, and cayenne or red pepper to taste
½ teaspoon dried dill or 4 fresh dill sprigs

Put all ingredients into container of an electric blender; process until puréed.

French Dressing Antillaise for Salads

½ cup olive oil
1 teaspoon salt
½ teaspoon freshly ground pepper
2 garlic cloves
  Tarragon, dill, or oregano to taste
5 parsley sprigs
2 scallions or green onions,
  finely chopped
1 tablespoon wine vinegar

1. Pour oil into a salad bowl; add remaining ingredients. With a pestle or wooden spoon, rub herbs against the side of the bowl and mix with oil.
2. For salad, marinate your choice of **celery pieces**, **chickpeas**, **onion slices**, **cherry tomatoes**, **sliced mushrooms**, **sliced cooked beets**, or **beans** (never more than two) in dressing for at least 1 hour before serving.
3. To serve, toss chilled **salad greens** with marinated vegetables.

Mayonnaise

2 egg yolks
½ teaspoon salt
¼ teaspoon white pepper
1 teaspoon prepared mustard
1 cup olive oil
1½ teaspoons vinegar*

Rinse a soup plate with hot water and dry well. Put egg yolks and seasoning into plate. Pour a few drops of oil over these ingredients and, with a fork or wooden spoon, stir in a slow circular motion until all the ingredients have been blended together. Continue the dripping of oil and the slow, even motion until ¼ cup oil has been blended in, then add ½ teaspoon vinegar, still stirring, then begin to pour the oil in a thin stream, never changing the pace of the beating. If the emulsion gets too thick and forms a ball, add a little more vinegar. To do it right takes about 20 minutes. The result is much richer than with the electric beater used at medium speed. When all the oil is blended in, finish with 1 teaspoon vinegar.

*The quality of the vinegar is important. Herb-flavored vinegar should be used to enhance certain dishes and salads.

Watercress Mayonnaise

Handful watercress, finely chopped
¾ cup Mayonnaise (page 64)
4 drops Tabasco

Blend all ingredients and serve with cold fish or shellfish.

Note: Dill, capers, chervil, or horseradish may be substituted for the watercress.

Herbal Mayonnaise Odette Mennesson

3 parsley sprigs
3 basil sprigs
2 fennel or dill sprigs
6 watercress sprigs
3 leaves Boston or Bibb lettuce
2 scallions or green onions
2 hard-cooked eggs
1 cup Mayonnaise (page 64)

Stem herbs, watercress, and lettuce. Chop very finely along with scallions and eggs. Blend in Mayonnaise.

2 cups

Bean Sauce

3 scallions or green onions, chopped
2 parsley sprigs
2 shallots
1 green hot pepper or
    6 dried Italian pepper pods
2 tablespoons peanut oil
2 cups dried red beans, rinsed
    Bouquet garni
2 quarts water (see Note)
1 small ham hock
1 cup cubed ham
    Salt and pepper to taste

1. In a mortar, pound to a paste the scallions, parsley, shallots, and hot pepper.
2. Heat oil in a Dutch oven over medium heat, add seasoning paste, beans, and bouquet garni. Stir until beans are lightly coated with oil.
3. Add water, ham hock, and cubed ham and bring to boiling. Cover and simmer 2 hours, or until beans are tender.
4. Remove ham hock. Process beans and juice in an electric blender or force through a food mill.
5. Return sauce to Dutch oven and bring to boiling. Season with salt and pepper. Serve warm over Caribbean Rice (page 59) or meats.

1½ quarts

Note: If using fresh beans, add only 1 quart water.

Four Thieves Vinegar

The "four thieves" are, like the bouquet garni, a standard combination of narrow-leaved basil, rosemary, sage, and marjoram commonly used in eighteenth-century French cuisine.

Several sprigs each of
    narrow-leaved basil, rosemary,
    sage, and majoram
10 cloves
1 cinnamon stick
10 peppercorns, cracked
2 garlic cloves
1 bay leaf
    Thyme sprig
2 tablespoons salt
8 dried Italian pepper pods
3½ cups wine vinegar
2 garlic cloves

1. Stem the basil, rosemary, sage, and majoram and put into a 1-quart jar along with the spices, 2 garlic cloves, bay leaf, thyme, salt, and pepper pods. Pour vinegar into jar; cover. Allow to stand 1 month in a sunny window, then strain through wet cheesecloth.
2. Put a garlic clove into each of 2 decorative 1-pint bottles; cover tightly.
3. Use for sauces and to make Condiments (page 66).

Condiments

Some people like their food very spicy, so on every table in the islands sits a bottle of pickled mixture of hot peppers and vegetables. A great deal of pride is taken in the coloring and general aspect of the condiment, as well as in the container which, in certain families, is of the most precious antique crystal.

1 medium head cabbage, very
    finely shredded
2 small heads cauliflower
    (tips of flowerets only)
1 cup frenched green beans
1 cup green onions (white part only)
1 cup thinly sliced small carrots
1 cucumber, diced
1 cup julienned red and green
    sweet pepper
  Snow peas (fresh or frozen),
    halved
  Small shallots
  Lime juice
6 peppercorns, cracked
2 cloves
2 bay leaves
2 cherry peppers (fresh or pickled)
4 small green hot peppers
    (fresh or pickled)
2 fresh cayenne pepper pods
    (if available)

1. Combine the vegetables.
2. Marinate desired number of shallots in lime juice 30 minutes, or until a deep purple color.
3. Drain vegetables and shallots well on paper towels. Arrange mixture decoratively in jars, then add spices and pepper to each so they can be seen from the outside.

DESSERTS

The most prized dessert for islanders is a tiny cup of delectable coffee: "Black as the devil, hot as hell, sweet as a Marabou woman" is the saying.

The Jesuits introduced coffee to the Antilles around 1720. The first coffee plantation was at Terrier Rouge, on a place named Caracoli. The café Caracoli achieved such instant fame at Versailles that by 1777 there existed 3,800 coffee plantations in the French colonies, each having an annual production of 20,000 pounds. The Caracoli of today ripens mostly on the wild-growing bushes on the small farms. The bean is small and greenish. The true connoisseur roasts only enough for daily family use. Beans are put in a *chaudière,* just enough to cover the bottom, and are roasted slowly until dark and glossy, brittle when hit with a spoon, and showing dark yellow in the center. The countrywomen generally add 2 teaspoons brown sugar to approximately 1 pound of coffee when roasting. These beans are then ground and slowly filtered through with boiling water. One and a half cups ground coffee make 6 demitasses; the old-fashioned way is to sweeten it with brown sugar, 1 heaping tablespoon to the small cup.

Blanc-mange, creams, and pâtisseries are reserved for grand occasions. The cakes are French in style and made from Génoise batter. Haiti, which knew American occupation from 1916 to 1934, has adapted a few baking powder doughs. There are popular sweets which are peddled up and down the streets of the towns to the cries of *"Bonbon Siro, Laco, Biski Yoyo, Lege-Lege."* The vendors, mostly young boys, carry a closed wooden box on their heads. They dole out their wares neatly with a fork onto a clean piece of paper.

The Duc de Praslin, who owned the Ile de la Tortue with his sister but never set foot on it, is supposed to have invented pralines and chocolate truffles, which he made from the produce of his plantation.

In Guadeloupe, on the Sunday set aside for Catholic First Communion, special cakes, macaroons, nougats, and pralines are brought to the church steps on large wooden trays for the communicants to partake of after the ceremony. The sweets are served with *cheaudeau,* a preparation which looks like a chocolate soup and is prepared with grated cocoa, milk, cinnamon, vanilla, the zest of a lime, 12 egg yolks and 10 large crumbled macaroons. In Martinique this public custom has disappeared, but in the homes of the communicants the *cheaudeau* is still served to the assembled friends and relatives.

Baked Bananas

6 ripe bananas
¼ cup lime juice
½ cup orange juice
¼ cup packed brown sugar
3 tablespoons amber rum
Cinnamon
Butter
1½ cups grated coconut

1. Peel bananas and coat them with lime juice to keep them from darkening. Cut bananas in half lengthwise and arrange in a well-buttered baking dish. Mix orange juice, brown sugar, and rum. Pour over bananas and sprinkle with cinnamon. Dot with butter and cover with grated coconut.
2. Bake at 400°F 12 to 15 minutes.

Banana Compote

½ cup sugar
½ cup apricot jam
1 cup water
6 ripe bananas
¼ cup unsalted butter

1. Combine sugar, jam, and water in a saucepan. Cook over medium heat until the syrup is heavy. Set aside.
2. Peel bananas and slice into ¼-inch pieces. Melt butter in a heavy skillet over medium heat and put in enough banana slices to cover bottom of skillet. Sauté until edges become golden. Pour reserved syrup over all bananas and boil uncovered over high heat until syrup is slightly thicker. Cool.
3. Pour into a crystal bowl, chill, and serve.

Banana Fan

4 ripe bananas
1 cup water
½ cup sugar
1 cup maraschino cherries
½ cup amber rum, warmed and
   flamed
1 cup whipped cream
¼ teaspoon vanilla extract

1. Peel bananas and halve them lengthwise. Arrange halves flat side down in the shape of an open fan on a round silver or glass dish.
2. Boil water and sugar together at a rolling boil 4 minutes. Add cherries, reduce heat, and simmer 2 minutes. Remove some of the cherries with a perforated spoon and arrange in a design on upper portion of fan.
3. Put the remaining fruit with syrup into an electric blender along with flamed rum; process until puréed. Or force mixture through a food mill. Spoon over upper part of fan.
4. Blend whipped cream and vanilla extract. Using a pastry bag and decorating tube, make a thick border around upper portion of fan to simulate lace. Serve well chilled.

Banana Fritters

1 cup all-purpose flour
1 teaspoon baking powder
⅛ teaspoon salt
1 egg, beaten
⅓ cup milk
1 teaspoon grated orange peel
¼ cup orange juice
4 ripe bananas
   Fat for deep frying,
      heated to 365°F
   Confectioners' sugar
   Orange Rum Sauce (page 85)

1. Sift flour, baking powder, and salt. Combine beaten egg and milk; add to dry ingredients along with orange peel and juice; mix until smooth.
2. Peel and slice bananas; stir into batter.
3. Drop by spoonfuls into heated fat and fry until golden. Drain on absorbent paper. Sprinkle with confectioners' sugar. Serve with the sauce.

Chestnuts with Coffee Cream

1 pound chestnuts
3 tablespoons brown sugar
Coffee Cream (page 83)

1. Slit shells of chestnuts. Simmer chestnuts, in water to cover, 5 minutes. While the chestnuts are still hot, discard shells and skins. Put nuts into boiling water with brown sugar and cook 30 minutes, or until tender. Drain and chill.
2. To serve, pile chestnuts into sherbet glasses. Spoon Coffee Cream over them.

Pineapple Ablaze

1 cup packed brown sugar
1 cup water
6 fresh pineapple slices
6 raisin bread slices with
    crusts trimmed
½ cup unsalted butter
6 tablespoons coarsely ground
    cashews
1 teaspoon cinnamon
½ cup amber rum

1. Combine brown sugar and water in a saucepan. Bring to boiling and boil rapidly until reduced to half its volume, Add pineapple and poach for 6 minutes. Remove pineapple and keep syrup warm.
2. Fry bread slices in butter in a skillet until golden.
3. Lay these croutons in a circle in a chafing dish. Top with pineapple slices and sprinkle with cashews and cinnamon. Spoon half the syrup into chafing dish pan. Warm rum, ignite, and pour, still flaming, over all.

6 servings

Pineapple Flan

3 cups pineapple juice
2 cups sugar
½ cup water
1 cup sugar
6 eggs
2 egg yolks

1. Combine pineapple juice and 2 cups sugar in a saucepan. Bring to a boil, then reduce heat and cook until a thin syrup is formed (about 5 minutes). Remove from heat, cool, and reserve.
2. Combine water and 1 cup sugar in a saucepan. Boil rapidly until it turns the color of maple syrup (5 to 7 minutes). Immediately remove from heat and pour it into a 1-quart mold, tilting mold until it is completely coated with caramel. Set aside to cool.
3. Beat eggs and yolks with the reserved pineapple syrup. Pour into mold. Set mold in a pan of hot water.
4. Bake at 325°F 1½ hours. Cool.
5. Chill thoroughly, then unmold on a serving platter.

About 12 servings

Pineapple Pyramids

2½ cups crushed Coconut Macaroons
    (page 77)
3 tablespoons amber rum
3 cups whipping cream
⅓ cup sugar
¾ cup chopped cashews
12 pineapple slices
12 whole cashews

1. Sprinkle crushed macaroons with rum.
2. Whip cream with sugar, one half at a time, until it stands in peaks. Fold crumbs and chopped cashews into the whipped cream.
3. Place 1 pineapple slice on each dessert plate, mound cream mixture in a pyramid, and put a cashew on top of each.

12 servings

Rum Pineapple Snow

1 small fresh fully ripe pineapple
4 egg whites
½ cup sugar
2 cups whipping cream
1 teaspoon vanilla extract
¾ cup amber rum
   Ladyfingers or leftover Génoise
   (page 74)

1. Pare pineapple and grate; keep grated pineapple separate from juice.
2. Beat egg whites until frothy; gradually add sugar while beating until meringue is thick and glossy.
3. Whip cream and blend in vanilla extract; fold into meringue along with as much grated pineapple and pineapple juice as meringue will hold and still pile softly.
4. Pour rum over ladyfingers and use to line sherbet glasses. Spoon in pineapple snow.

Pineapple Boat

1 small pineapple
2 cups whipping cream
1 cup sugar
1 tablespoon lime juice
½ cup whipped cream mixed with
   chopped flaked coconut
   Chopped cashews

1. Cut pineapple in half lengthwise, a little off center. Remove pulp, keeping larger shell intact, and discard core. Chop pineapple finely or process in an electric blender. Measure 2 cups of pineapple and juice. Add to whipping cream along with sugar and lime juice.
2. Cut the leafy top off the pineapple shell and reserve for decoration. Spoon pineapple mixture into the shell and freeze until firm.
3. To serve, pipe large rosettes of the whipped cream around the shell and sprinkle with cashews. Decorate with leafy top.

Baked Pineapple

1 large sugarloaf pineapple
1 banana, peeled and thinly sliced
¼ cup packed brown sugar
⅓ cup amber rum

1. Cut top from pineapple and remove pulp from inside the top. Reserve leafy top. With a grapefruit knife, remove the core and pulp from the pineapple, being careful to leave a ¼-inch layer of flesh inside the rind to keep juice in during baking.
2. Dice the pineapple pulp and mix with banana and brown sugar in a bowl. Warm rum, ignite it, and, when the flame subsides, pour over fruit mixture. Fill pineapple shell with fruit; replace top, moisten with water, and wrap in foil. Secure top with a few wooden picks. Set upright in oven in a deep casserole.
3. Bake at 350°F 25 minutes. Remove foil and serve hot.

Oranges Packed in Rum

18 small unblemished juicy oranges
4 pounds brown sugar
1 quart cold water
2 egg whites
1½ cups ice water
1 quart amber rum

1. Wash and dry oranges. Prick them all over with a darning needle and drop them into a pan of cold water. Let them stand 15 minutes to remove some of the oil. Wipe oranges, then put them into boiling water and heat until they are soft (about 5 minutes).
2. Mix brown sugar, cold water, and egg whites in a large saucepot; stir until sugar is dissolved. Bring to the boiling point while stirring. Add ice water and again bring to boiling point; reduce heat and simmer 5 minutes, carefully skimming. When syrup is clear, add oranges and bring to a boil, cool slightly, and again bring to a boil.
3. Remove oranges with a slotted spoon and put them on a platter. Cover syrup and oranges; let stand overnight.
4. The next morning, return the fruit to the syrup and bring to a boil, cool slightly, and again bring to a boil.
5. Pack oranges in five or six 2-quart Mason jars. Mix the syrup with an equal amount of rum; pour over oranges, filling jars. Seal at once. Store 1 month before use.
6. Serve with ice cream.

Pineapple Fritters

1 ripe pineapple, pared and cored
1 cup Barbancourt rum or other
   amber rum
¾ cup sugar
2 cups all-purpose flour
1 cup light beer
2 egg whites
1 egg yolk
   Fat for deep frying,
      heated to 365°F
   Pineapple Sauce (page 83)

1. Cube the pineapple pulp and combine with rum and sugar in a bowl. Marinate for 2 hours, turning occasionally.
2. Combine remaining ingredients to make a thick, smooth batter.
3. Drain and dry pineapple. Dip pineapple cubes in batter to coat.
4. Fry pineapple cubes, a few at a time, in heated fat until golden brown (about 30 seconds).
5. Drain on absorbent paper and serve warm with the sauce.

Tutti-Frutti Barbancourt

2 quarts strawberries
1 quart honey
4 cinnamon sticks
32 whole cloves
¼ cup grated orange peel
¼ cup grated lime peel
   Mangoes, peeled and cut in pieces
   Bananas, sliced
   Pineapple, cubed
   Barbancourt rum or other
     amber rum

1. Cook strawberries in honey and enough water to cover over low heat 5 minutes. Skim thoroughly; spoon an equal amount into each of four 2-quart wide-mouthed Mason jars. Put into each jar 1 cinnamon stick, 8 cloves, and 1 tablespoon each orange and lime peel. When cool, fill jars with desired amount of remaining fruit and rum. Stir, cover tightly, and refrigerate 3 months.
2. Serve tutti-frutti over ice cream or plain, with cookies.

8 quarts tutti-frutti

Spiked Watermelon

1 large ripe watermelon
2 cups amber rum

1. Cut a hole 2½ inches wide and 2 inches deep in the watermelon rind. Pour rum through hole and replace rind.
2. Chill 24 hours. Serve ice-cold slices.

Gâteau du Mardi-Gras

Meringue Circles:
3 egg whites
½ teaspoon almond extract
¼ teaspoon salt
¾ cup firmly packed brown sugar
½ cup chopped cashews
1 teaspoon multicolored nonpareilles
   or colored sugar

Filling:
1 package (6 ounces) semisweet
   chocolate pieces
1 package (8 ounces) cream cheese
1 tablespoon milk
1 teaspoon vanilla extract
⅛ teaspoon salt
¾ cup firmly packed brown sugar
½ cup whipping cream, whipped

1. For meringue circles, cut four 8-inch circles of brown or waxed paper.
2. Beat egg whites with almond extract and ¼ teaspoon salt until light and foamy. Add brown sugar gradually while beating until stiff and glossy. Fold in cashews.
3. Spread meringue on paper circles; slide onto cookie sheets. Sprinkle top of 1 circle with nonpareilles.
4. Bake at 300°F 35 minutes. Peel off paper from meringue circles.
5. For filling, melt chocolate pieces over hot, not boiling, water. Cool about 10 minutes.
6. Beat cream cheese until creamy. Blend in milk, vanilla extract, and salt. Add brown sugar gradually, beating until smooth. Add cooled melted chocolate and blend well. Fold in whipped cream.
7. Spread a fourth of the filling on each of the 3 plain meringue circles. Stack circles and top with decorated circle. Cover sides with remaining filling. Chill overnight.

12 to 15 servings

Génoise

This light cake is something quite different from "American cake," and is well worth the effort.

1 cup sugar
6 eggs
2 teaspoons vanilla extract
    Grated peel of 1 lime
1 cup all-purpose flour
¼ cup clarified butter

1. Combine sugar, eggs, vanilla extract, and grated peel in the top of a double boiler. Beat with an electric mixer over hot water for 15 minutes, or until light and fluffy. Remove from heat. Continue beating until mixture is cooled and has reached the ribbon stage. (The mixture should flow in ribbons and softly peak.)
2. Sift the flour onto the cooled mixture a fourth at a time; fold in gently after each addition. Fold in clarified butter.
3. Pour the batter into 2 greased and floured 9-inch round layer cake pans.
4. Bake at 325°F about 25 minutes, or until cake tests done.
5. Cool on racks. Frost cooled layers with **Rich Chocolate Frosting (page 75)** or **Italian Meringue (page 77)**.

One 9-inch layer cake

Coconut Génoise: Follow recipe for Génoise, using only ¾ cup flour and adding ½ **cup freshly grated coconut or flaked coconut, chopped.** Pour batter into a greased 15x10x1-inch baking pan. Bake at 325°F about 20 minutes, or until cake tests done. Cool on a rack. Cut cooled cake into 2 layers. Fill with desired amount of **Rum Cream (page 83)** mixed with ⅓ **cup grated or flaked coconut.** Frost with **Italian Meringue (page 77)**. Decorate with **red-tinted grated coconut.**

Orange Cake *(Gâteau à l'Orange)*

1 cup butter
1 cup sugar
3 egg yolks
2 cups sifted all-purpose flour
1 teaspoon baking powder
1 teaspoon baking soda
1 cup milk
1 teaspoon lime juice
1 tablespoon grated
    orange peel
¾ cup cashews, chopped
3 egg whites
    Pinch salt
½ cup orange juice
½ cup corn syrup
¼ cup rum

1. Cream butter with sugar until light and fluffy. Beat in egg yolks.
2. Sift flour with baking powder and baking soda. Mix milk and lime juice. Add dry ingredients alternately with milk to creamed mixture, beating until blended after each addition. Mix in orange peel and cashews.
3. Beat egg whites and salt to stiff, not dry, peaks. Fold into batter.
4. Turn batter into a buttered and lightly floured 9-inch tube pan.
5. Bake at 350°F 40 minutes.
6. Mix orange juice, corn syrup, and rum. While cake is still hot in the pan, pour orange juice mixture over it.

Marabou Cake

4 ounces (4 squares) unsweetened
    chocolate, halved
¾ cup milk
1 cup all-purpose flour
1 teaspoon baking powder
¼ cup amber rum
4 egg yolks
2 cups packed dark brown sugar
4 egg whites
⅓ cup whipping cream, whipped
½ cup crushed Coconut Macaroons
    (page 77)
    Rich Chocolate Frosting
    Slivered blanched almonds

1. Put chocolate and milk into the top of a double boiler. Set over simmering water until chocolate is melted. Set aside to cool.
2. Sift flour and baking powder together into a bowl.
3. Mix rum with melted chocolate. Stir into flour in bowl.
4. Beat egg yolks, gradually adding brown sugar. Add to flour-chocolate mixture.
5. Beat egg whites until stiff, not dry, peaks form. Lightly fold into batter. Pour batter into 2 greased and floured 8-inch round layer cake pans.
6. Bake at 350°F 25 to 30 minutes, or until cake tests done.
7. Cool about 10 minutes. Gently run a spatula around sides of pan. Invert cake layers onto racks and cool completely.
8. For filling, combine whipped cream and crushed Coconut Macaroons. Place a cake layer on a serving plate. Cover with filling. Top with second cake layer. Frost with Rich Chocolate Frosting. Decorate with slivered blanched almonds.

One 2-layer 8-inch cake

Rich Chocolate Frosting

1 package (6 ounces) semisweet
    chocolate pieces
⅓ cup strong black coffee
½ cup butter or margarine,
    cut in pieces

1. Put chocolate pieces and coffee in a heavy saucepan. Set over low heat and stir constantly just until chocolate is melted.
2. Pour mixture into a bowl. Add butter, piece by piece, beating until mixture is smooth.
3. Chill until frosting is of spreading consistency.

About 1½ cups frosting

Haitian Upside-down Cake *(Gâteau Pistaches)*

Topping:
    6 tablespoons butter, melted
    ½ cup firmly packed dark brown
        sugar
    ¼ cup light corn syrup
    1 cup chopped pistachios or peanuts
Cake:
    4 ounces (4 squares) unsweetened
        chocolate
    6 tablespoons butter
    1¼ cups sugar
    2 egg yolks
    1 teaspoon vanilla extract
    2 cups all-purpose flour
    1 tablespoon baking powder
    1½ cups milk
    2 egg whites, beaten stiff, but
        not dry

1. For topping, blend butter, brown sugar, and corn syrup, then add nuts and mix well.
2. Spread nut mixture over bottom of a greased 13x9-inch baking pan.
3. For cake, melt chocolate over hot, not boiling, water.
4. Cream butter with sugar thoroughly. Beat in egg yolks, vanilla extract, and melted chocolate.
5. Sift flour with baking powder. Alternately add flour mixture with milk to the chocolate mixture, beating until blended after each addition. Fold in beaten egg white. Turn batter into pan over nut mixture.
6. Bake at 350°F about 45 minutes. Invert on a board or platter. If necessary, spread nut mixture evenly over the cake. Cool; serve cut in squares.

One 13x9-inch cake

Superlative Banana Cake *(Figues Meringuées)*

Yellow, ripe bananas are called bananes-figues *in contrast to the yellow plantain which is known as* banane mûre.

1 cup Pineapple Cream (page 83)
1 sponge cake, homemade or commercial
2 bananas
3 egg whites
3 tablespoons confectioners' sugar

1. Prepare and chill Pineapple Cream.
2. Slice sponge cake to make two layers.
3. Peel bananas and slice on the diagonal. Mix with Pineapple Cream. Spread half of mixture over each cake layer. Put cake together.
4. Beat egg whites until frothy. Add confectioners' sugar gradually, beating until peaks form. Frost sides and top of cake.
5. Bake at 450°F until delicately browned. Serve hot or cold.

Wedding Cake

The decoration of island cakes is an imaginative process in the grand baroque style. There should be butter-cream roses, and cornucopias spilling silver sprinkles. The cake is often placed on a large mirror. Toy models of all the status symbols which are wished for the couple are dipped in icing and placed around the cake.

1 cup unsalted butter
2 cups firmly packed dark brown sugar
12 egg yolks
¼ cup dark molasses
4 cups all-purpose flour
2 teaspoons nutmeg
1 teaspoon cinnamon
1 teaspoon cloves
½ cup dark rum
4 cups dark raisins
3 cups currants
3 cups slivered almonds
½ cup chopped citron
½ cup chopped figs
12 egg whites
Italian Meringue (page 77)

1. Cream butter with brown sugar until fluffy and light. Beat in egg yolks and molasses.
2. Sift flour with spices. Alternately add with rum to creamed mixture, beating until blended after each addition. Mix in fruit and nuts.
3. Beat egg whites to soft peaks. Fold into cake batter.
4. Butter a 12-inch cake pan and fill two thirds full with batter. Fill a well-buttered 6-inch round deep cake pan or coffee can with remaining batter.
5. Bake at 300°F 1½ hours, or until cake tests done. Remove cakes from pans. Cool thoroughly.
6. Frost and decorate cake with desired amount of Italian Meringue.

Italian Meringue

2 cups sugar
1 cup water
2 egg whites
1 teaspoon cream of tartar
⅛ teaspoon salt
1 teaspoon lime juice
1 teaspoon vanilla extract

1. Combine sugar and water in a heavy saucepan. Cook covered over hot water for 3 minutes, or until the steam has washed down any crystals which may have formed on the sides. Uncover and bring to the soft crack stage (240°F). Remove from heat.
2. Beat egg whites, cream of tartar, and salt until soft peaks are formed. Pour the hot syrup slowly into the egg white, beating constantly until the icing is soft and meringue-like.
3. Stir in lime juice and vanilla extract.

2 cups

Note: This icing dries on the cake and should not be refrigerated.

Coconut Macaroons

4 egg whites
½ teaspoon vanilla extract
1 cup confectioners' sugar
½ cup all-purpose flour
2 cups freshly grated or chopped flaked coconut

1. Beat egg whites until rounded peaks are formed. Mix in vanilla extract. Add sugar gradually, beating until stiff, not dry, peaks form. Fold in flour and coconut.
2. Drop by tablespoonfuls 1 inch apart on a buttered and floured cookie sheet.
3. Bake at 350°F 10 to 15 minutes, or until lightly browned.

About 2½ dozen

Plantation Macaroons: Follow recipe for Coconut Macaroons. When cool, put 2 macaroons together, like a sandwich, with a filling of Rich Chocolate Frosting (page 75). Roll in **grated** or **flaked coconut**.

Fresh Pineapple Cake Ring
with Creole Macaroon Cream

½ cup butter
1 teaspoon vanilla extract
½ cup sugar
1 egg, beaten
1½ cups sifted cake flour
2 teaspoons baking powder
½ teaspoon salt
½ cup pineapple juice
¼ cup butter
½ cup packed brown sugar
6 slices fresh pineapple, halved
1 cup whipping cream
2 tablespoons confectioners' sugar
2 tablespoons rum
1½ cups coarsely crushed Coconut
    Macaroons (page 77)
    Silver sprinkles

1. Cream ½ cup butter with vanilla extract and sugar until fluffy. Add beaten egg and beat thoroughly.
2. Sift flour with baking powder and salt. Add dry ingredients alternately with pineapple juice to creamed mixture, beating until blended after each addition.
3. Melt ¼ cup butter in a small saucepan over low heat. Add brown sugar and stir until blended. Spread mixture in bottom of a 1½-quart ring mold. Press pineapple half-slices into brown sugar mixture. Turn batter into mold and spread evenly.
4. Bake at 350°F 30 minutes.
5. Loosen cake from mold. Cover with a serving plate and invert; allow mold to remain over cake 1 or 2 minutes. Lift mold off. Cool cake.
6. Whip cream and beat in confectioners' sugar and rum. Fold in crushed macaroons.
7. To serve, pile macaroon cream into center of ring. Decorate with silver sprinkles.

Coconut Praline

1 cup water
1 tablespoon vanilla extract
  Peel of 1 lime
2 cups freshly grated or chopped
  flaked coconut
½ cup whipping cream
1 cup firmly packed brown sugar

1. Combine water, vanilla extract, and lime peel in a saucepan. Bring to a boil over medium heat, reduce heat, and simmer 5 minutes. Discard lime peel. Cool mixture slightly. Add coconut, cream, and brown sugar; mix well. Cook over medium heat, stirring constantly, until mixture thickens and leaves bottom and sides of pan (15 to 20 minutes). Spread in a shallow 3-quart dish. Cool, then chill.
2. To serve, cut into 2-inch squares.

Anispraline: Follow recipe for Coconut Praline; omit lime peel and add 1 **tablespoon rum** and desired amounts of **aniseed**, **grated lemon peel**, and **raisins**.

Rum Omelet

1 tablespoon brown sugar
  Grated peel of 1 orange
4 eggs, beaten
2 tablespoons butter or margarine
1 tablespoon sugar
¼ cup amber rum

1. Add brown sugar and grated orange peel to beaten eggs.
2. Melt butter over high heat in a large skillet. Add the egg mixture. Immediately use a fork or spoon to push the edges of the thickened egg mass towards the center, so the liquid fills the vacant spaces. Repeat this procedure until the eggs are cooked but still soft. Remove from heat.
3. Place omelet, folded in half, on an oven-proof platter. Sprinkle sugar on omelet surface. Broil 3 to 4 inches from heat, until sugar caramelizes.
4. Heat rum in a small saucepan. Ignite rum and pour over the omelet.

2 servings

Haitian Pumpkin Flan

Caramel:
  1 cup water
1½ cups sugar
Custard:
  1 egg
  2 egg yolks
⅔ cup sugar
1½ cups half-and-half
  2 cups cooked pumpkin purée
½ teaspoon salt
½ teaspoon ground ginger
¼ teaspoon cinnamon
1 tablespoon grated lime peel
  Caramel Sauce (page 84)

1. For caramel, put water and sugar into a heavy skillet and cook until syrup is golden and reaches the hard-crack stage (forms threads which are hard and brittle in very cold water). Pour the caramel into a 1-quart ring mold, tilting the mold to coat it evenly. Set the mold in ice to harden coating; do not refrigerate.
2. For custard, beat egg, egg yolks, sugar, and half-and-half. Add pumpkin, salt, ginger, cinnamon, and lime peel; mix well. Pour mixture into caramel-coated mold. Put mold into a pan of hot water.
3. Bake at 300°F 45 minutes, or until the custard is set and a knife inserted near center comes out clean. Cool, then chill the flan.
4. Unmold chilled flan on a chilled serving plate. Serve with Caramel Sauce.

Banana Pudding

3	white bread slices with crusts trimmed
1½	cups hot milk
1	egg
½	cup packed brown sugar
¼	cup butter
	Grated peel and juice of 1 lime
1	tablespoon amber rum
½	teaspoon vanilla extract
⅛	teaspoon cinnamon
1	cup water
1½	cups sugar
4	fully ripe bananas

1. Soak bread in hot milk, then mix and mash to a paste. Add egg, brown sugar, butter, lime peel and juice, rum, vanilla extract, and cinnamon; mix well.
2. Boil water and sugar over high heat until syrup is the color of maple syrup. Immediately remove from heat and pour into a 1-quart mold, tilting and rotating to spread the caramel evenly on the sides and bottom of mold. Chill the caramel.
3. Meanwhile, mash bananas to a smooth purée and stir in bread mixture. Turn into the mold.
4. Bake at 300°F 30 minutes. Unmold and serve hot or cold.

Sweet Potato Loaf (Pain Patate)

5	medium sweet potatoes, preferably of the purple variety
2	ripe bananas
1	cup half-and-half
1	cup packed brown sugar
½	teaspoon cinnamon
½	teaspoon nutmeg
¼	teaspoon cloves
1½	teaspoons vanilla extract
½	teaspoon freshly grated ginger root
2	tablespoons unsalted butter, melted
	Orange Rum Sauce (page 85)

1. Pare, then grate sweet potatoes. Peel and mash bananas and mix with sweet potato along with half-and-half and brown sugar. Add spices, vanilla extract, ginger root, and melted butter; mix well. Turn mixture into a shallow 3-quart baking dish.
2. Bake at 350°F 50 minutes. Cool and serve with sauce.

Sweet Potato Pudding

1	cup raisins
½	cup amber rum
3	cups Coconut Milk (page 86)
5	medium sweet potatoes
2	tablespoons butter
1	tablespoon vanilla extract
1½	teaspoons cinnamon
1½	teaspoons nutmeg
½	teaspoon cloves
3	eggs, beaten
	Orange Rum Sauce (page 85) (optional)

1. Marinate raisins in rum. Prepare Coconut Milk; reserve.
2. Boil sweet potatoes in their skins 25 minutes, or until tender. Cool them, then peel and purée, adding butter, vanilla extract, cinnamon, nutmeg, and cloves. Mix in Coconut Milk, beaten egg, and raisins with rum.
3. Grease a 2-quart pudding mold and pour in sweet potato mixture.
4. Bake at 350°F 35 minutes. Unmold and serve hot or cold with sauce, if desired.

Papaya Custard (Flan de Papaye Renversé)

1 quart fresh or canned papaya pulp
1 cup Toasted Coconut (page 80)
1 quart half-and-half
1 vanilla bean piece (4 inches)
6 eggs
¼ cup sugar
Salt
Grated peel and juice of 1
large orange
1 cup Guava Jelly (page 53)

1. Mix papaya pulp with coconut. Spread in bottom of a buttered shallow 3-quart baking dish. Set aside.
2. Scald half-and-half with vanilla bean. Beat eggs, adding sugar and a little salt. Pour in scalded half-and-half while beating. Stir in orange peel and juice. Pour over fruit in baking dish. Set dish in a pan of hot water.
3. Bake at 350°F 35 minutes, or until a knife inserted near center comes out clean. Cool.
4. When cool, loosen from baking dish and invert on a chilled platter.
5. Melt jelly and pour around custard.

Vanilla Soufflé

3 tablespoons unsalted butter
2 tablespoons flour
1 cup milk
½ cup sugar
¼ teaspoon salt
1 vanilla bean piece (4 inches)
4 egg yolks, beaten
5 egg whites, beaten to soft peaks
Sugar

1. Melt butter in a saucepan over medium heat. Blend in flour. Add milk gradually while beating with a whisk. Add ½ cup sugar, salt, and vanilla bean piece; mix well. Cook and stir until thick and smooth.
2. Remove from heat and cool. Stir in beaten egg yolk; beat well. Fold in beaten egg white.
3. Butter a 1½-quart soufflé dish and sprinkle with sugar. Pour in batter. Set the dish in a pan of hot water.
4. Bake at 375°F 25 to 30 minutes. The center should still be a little softer than the sides, in the French-approved style.
5. This is often served with any of the fruit sauces, Rum Sauce, or Haitian Chocolate Rum Sauce (pages 86, 85).

Coffee Soufflé: Follow recipe for Vanilla Soufflé, substituting ½ **cup strong coffee** for ½ cup milk.

Chocolate Soufflé: Follow recipe for Vanilla Soufflé; add **2 ounces (2 squares) unsweetened chocolate** to the thickened sauce and stir until chocolate is melted and sauce thoroughly blended. Proceed as directed.

Molded Coconut Cream

2 envelopes unflavored gelatin
½ cup sugar
½ cup whipping cream
2 cups Coconut Milk (page 86)
⅛ teaspoon salt
2 teaspoons vanilla extract
1½ cups whipping cream
Toasted Coconut
Coconut Chocolate Sauce
(page 84)

1. Mix gelatin and sugar in a heavy saucepan and stir in ½ cup cream. Set over low heat and stir until gelatin and sugar are dissolved. Remove from heat and add Coconut Milk, salt, and vanilla extract; stir well. Chill until slightly thickened.
2. Beat remaining cream until it piles softly. Fold into gelatin mixture.
3. Rinse a 5-cup mold with cold water and pour cream mixture into it. Chill until firm.
4. Unmold on a chilled platter. Garnish with coconut and serve with sauce.

Toasted Coconut: Spread desired amount of **freshly grated coconut** in a shallow pan. Heat in 350°F oven about 20 minutes, or until light brown; stir frequently.

Chocolate Charlotte

14 ladyfingers, split
½ cup tea
½ cup amber rum
1 envelope unflavored gelatin
¼ cup milk
½ cup hot coffee
1 package (6 ounces) semisweet
      chocolate pieces
1 tablespoon sugar
2 egg yolks
1 heaping cup crushed ice
1 cup whipping cream
    Whipping cream, whipped

1. Line an oiled 5-cup mold with ladyfingers.
2. Mix tea with rum and moisten ladyfingers with the mixture.
3. In an electric blender, soften gelatin in milk. Add coffee, chocolate pieces, and sugar; blend 10 seconds, or until chocolate is smooth. Add egg yolks, crushed ice, and cream; blend 20 seconds. Pour into the mold over ladyfingers. Use remaining ladyfingers to cover the cream.
4. Chill overnight. Unmold on a serving dish. Make a whipped cream border around base of mold, using a pastry bag and tube.

Kirsch Banana Sherbet Josephine

4 all-yellow bananas
6 tablespoons kirsch
¾ cup sugar
    Pinch salt
⅛ teaspoon cinnamon
1 egg white, beaten stiff but not dry
2 cups cold skim milk

1. Mash bananas to make 2 cups purée. Blend in kirsch, sugar, salt, and cinnamon; fold in beaten egg white. Gradually add skim milk while stirring.
2. Pour into refrigerator tray and freeze until firm.

Mango Sherbet

1 cup sugar
1 quart water
5 cups coarsely chopped mango
¼ cup lime juice
3 egg whites, beaten stiff but not dry

1. Combine sugar and water in a saucepan. Heat rapidly, stirring until sugar is dissolved; reserve.
2. Purée mango in an electric blender with lime juice. There should be 4 cups purée. Blend reserved syrup and purée.
3. Cool, then freeze in refrigerator trays to the mushy stage.
4. Blend beaten egg white with partially frozen mixture. Freeze until firm.

Mocha Mousse

8 ounces (8 squares) unsweetened
    chocolate
⅔ cup Coffee Extract (page 86)
2 cups whipping cream
½ cup sugar
    Coconut Chocolate Sauce
        (page 84)

1. Put chocolate and Coffee Extract into a saucepan. Stir over low heat until chocolate is blended with coffee. Cool.
2. Whip cream and gradually add sugar, continuing to beat until cream holds its shape. Fold in cooled chocolate mixture. Pour into a mold and freeze without stirring.
3. Serve mousse with the sauce.

Tropical Ice Creams

Choice of ice cream mixture
    (see below)
4½ pounds coarse salt
10 pounds cracked ice

1. Prepare and chill ice cream mixture.
2. Fill freezer can two thirds full with the mix. In the ice cream freezer, pack the can in a mixture of salt and ice. Crank until paddles stop, then remove paddles and pack the ice cream down in the can.
3. Cover can and insulate it with newspapers or a blanket until serving time, or about 30 minutes.

Orange, Lime, Pineapple, Granadilla, and Soursop Creams: Make fruit juices as concentrated as possible and a little sweeter than for drinking. Mix **4 cups fruit juice** with **2 cups whipping cream**. Mix in **2 teaspoons vanilla extract**.

Mango Ice Cream: Purée enough fully ripe **mango pieces** in an electric blender or force pieces through a food mill to make 4 cups purée. Mix purée with **1 cup whipping cream**, **1 tablespoon vanilla extract**, and **1 cup honey**.

Coconut Ice Cream: Add **2 cups whipping cream** to **4 cups Coconut Milk (page 86)**, **2 teaspoons vanilla extract**, and, if desired, grated coconut pulp.

Coffee and Rum Ice Cream: Blend into **1 cup whipping cream** either **2 cups Coffee Cream (page 83)** and **½ cup amber rum**, warmed and flamed; or **2 cups Rum Cream (page 83)** and **2 tablespoons Coffee Extract (page 86)**.

Frozen Rum Cream

8 egg yolks
½ cup sugar
6 egg whites, stiffly beaten
3 cups whipped cream
1 cup amber rum
    Rum-flavored whipped cream
    Maraschino cherries (optional)

1. Beat egg yolks and sugar until mixture is thick and pale yellow. Fold in beaten egg whites and whipped cream. Add rum very gradually while stirring. Turn cream into deep refrigerator trays. Freeze without stirring 8 hours.
2. Serve in sherbet glasses topped with dollops of rum-flavored whipped cream and, if desired, maraschino cherries.

Pineapple Cream

1 pineapple, pared, sliced, and cored
2 tablespoons amber rum
½ cup butter or margarine
6 tablespoons sugar
1 tablespoon flour
6 egg yolks

1. Cube pineapple pulp and put with rum into the top of a double boiler over boiling water.
2. Beat remaining ingredients together about 5 minutes.
3. Pour the cream mixture over the pineapple cubes and mix well. Cook and stir over boiling water about 6 minutes, or until thickened.
4. Pour into small bowls or **pots de crème** cups and chill before serving.

About 3 cups

Coffee Cream

4 cups milk
2 tablespoons Coffee Extract
    (page 86)
3 tablespoons cornstarch
6 egg yolks, beaten
¾ cup sugar
1 tablespoon butter or margarine
¼ cup whipping cream

1. Combine ½ cup of the milk, Coffee Extract, and cornstarch. Beat in egg yolks. Set aside.
2. Put the remaining milk, sugar, and butter into the top of a metal double boiler. Bring to a boil over direct heat.
3. Half fill the bottom of the double boiler with water; bring to boiling. Place the top of the double boiler over the bottom pan.
4. Add the reserved milk-and-egg mixture to the top pan while stirring. Cook over medium heat, stirring until the custard thickens and coats the spoon.
5. Cool custard, then add cream. Pour into a large bowl or individual custard cups. Serve chilled.

Rum Cream: Follow recipe for Coffee Cream, omitting Coffee Extract and cream. Heat ¼ **cup amber rum** in a small saucepan. Ignite rum and stir it into the thickened custard. Serve chilled.

Lime Fluff

4 cups milk
2 tablespoons cornstarch
¾ cup sugar
1 tablespoon butter or margarine
6 egg yolks, beaten
1 tablespoon grated lime peel
2 tablespoons lime juice
6 egg whites

1. Mix ½ cup milk and cornstarch. Set aside.
2. Place in the top of a double boiler the remaining 3½ cups milk, sugar, and butter. Bring to a boil over direct heat.
3. Half fill the bottom of the double boiler with water; bring to boiling. Place the top of the double boiler over the bottom pan.
4. Add the reserved milk mixture and egg yolks to the boiling mixture while stirring. Cook over medium heat, stirring until it is thick and coats a spoon (about 5 minutes).
5. Stir in lime peel and juice. Pour mixture into a bowl. Set bowl in a larger bowl filled with ice and water to cool the mixture.
6. Beat egg whites until stiff, not dry, peaks are formed. Fold into cooled mixture.
7. Spoon into individual cups. Serve chilled.

About 10 servings

Crêpes Antillaises

  1 cup all-purpose flour
  ¼ teaspoon salt
  4 eggs
1¾ cups milk
  ¼ cup amber rum
  1 tablespoon butter, melted
1½ teaspoons butter
     Guava Jelly (page 53)
  1 cup chopped pineapple
  1 cup chopped banana
  1 tablespoon grated lime peel
  ½ cup grated coconut or chopped
       flaked coconut
  2 tablespoons unsalted butter
  ½ cup Guava Jelly
  ½ cup amber rum

1. Mix flour and salt. Beat eggs with milk and ¼ cup rum. Add the flour mixture gradually, then melted butter, beating until smooth. Refrigerate 1 hour.
2. Heat a 9-inch skillet until a drop of water on surface evaporates at once. Grease skillet with 1½ teaspoons butter. Add enough batter to coat bottom, rotating the skillet to spread batter. Bake until dry on top, then turn with a spatula. To obtain an even color on the reverse side, hold skillet an inch above high heat and shake it gently so crêpe slides back and forth. When crêpe is golden brown, slide it onto a hot platter. Prepare more crêpes with remaining batter, piling crêpes one on top of another; keep warm in an open oven.
3. Spread crêpes lightly with Guava Jelly.
4. Mix pineapple, banana, lime peel, and coconut. Spoon some filling in center of each crêpe. Fold one side of each crêpe over the other and then fold ends to make a square package.
5. Melt unsalted butter and ½ cup Guava Jelly in bottom of a chafing dish. Place crêpes in this sauce. Warm ½ cup rum, ignite it, and, while still flaming, pour over crêpes.

16 crêpes

Caramel Sauce

1½ cups sugar
  1 cup water
  ¼ cup hot water
  1 tablespoon butter

1. Put sugar and 1 cup water into a heavy saucepan and bring to a boil. Boil, stirring constantly, until syrup is golden.
2. Remove from heat and stir in hot water and butter.
3. Serve hot.

About 1½ cups

Coconut Chocolate Sauce

  4 ounces (4 squares) semisweet
       chocolate
1½ cups Coconut Milk (page 86)
  1 teaspoon vanilla extract

1. Combine chocolate and ¼ cup Coconut Milk in a saucepan. Stir over low heat until chocolate is melted. Gradually add the remaining Coconut Milk, stirring until smooth and blended.
2. Remove from heat and mix in vanilla extract.

About 2 cups

Haitian Chocolate Rum Sauce

1 cup Coffee Extract (page 86)
4 ounces dark sweet Swiss chocolate
1 ounce (1 square) unsweetened
    chocolate
1 cup amber rum

1. Combine Coffee Extract and chocolates in a heavy saucepan. Cook over low heat, stirring constantly, until chocolate is melted.
2. Heat rum, ignite it, and when the flames subside, stir into the chocolate mixture.
3. Serve hot over cake.

About 2 cups

Orange Coconut Filling

1 cup sugar
½ cup orange juice
3½ tablespoons cornstarch
3 tablespoons lime juice
2 tablespoons butter
2 tablespoons water
    Grated peel of 1 orange
1 egg, slightly beaten
¾ cup freshly grated or chopped
    flaked coconut

1. Combine all the ingredients except the coconut in a saucepan. Cook over low heat, stirring constantly, about 10 minutes or until thick and clear; do not boil.
2. Remove from heat and stir in coconut. Cool before using.

About 1 cup

Orange Rum Sauce

1½ cups orange juice
½ cup amber rum
    Sugar to taste
1 tablespoon butter
1 tablespoon cornstarch
½ teaspoon grated orange peel

1. Combine orange juice, rum, and sugar in a small saucepan. Bring to a boil.
2. Mix butter and cornstarch and add to sauce. Cook until thickened. Remove from heat. Mix in orange peel.
3. Cool before serving.

About 2 cups

Pineapple Sauce

1½ cups cubed pineapple,
    canned or fresh
½ cup sugar
¼ cup rum, flamed
    Pineapple juice
½ cup water
1 tablespoon cornstarch

1. Process pineapple, sugar, and rum in an electric blender until completely smooth. Add pineapple juice if more liquid is needed.
2. Turn pineapple mixture into a small saucepan and bring to a boil.
3. Mix water and cornstarch, stir into mixture in saucepan, and cook until sauce is slightly thickened.

1⅔ cups

Rum Sauce

1 cup milk
1½ teaspoons vanilla extract
3 egg yolks
½ cup sugar
2 tablespoons amber rum

1. Scald milk with vanilla extract in the top of a double boiler over boiling water.
2. Beat egg yolks and sugar together in a small bowl. Stir into milk, using a wire whip. Cook until mixture is thick and coats a spoon.
3. Remove from heat and stir in rum.

About 1 cup

Coffee Extract *(Essence de Café)*

5 cups water
1½ cups ground coffee

1. Prepare very strong coffee using water and ground coffee.
2. Pour brewed coffee into a large saucepan. Bring to a boil; simmer 30 minutes. Cool.
3. Store in a tightly covered container and use to flavor custard, buttercream, and ice cream.

About ½ cup extract

Coconut Milk

1 fresh coconut
2 cups boiling water

1. Open coconut, discarding liquid. With a sharp paring knife, remove the meat in chunks and grate it (see Note). Pour boiling water over grated coconut and let stand 4 hours.
2. Place a sieve over a bowl, turn grated coconut into sieve, and press out the liquid. Reserve grated coconut, if desired, to toast in the oven and use to decorate desserts and salads.

About 2 cups

Note: If you have an electric blender, coarsely chop coconut meat and process with boiling water a small amount at a time.

BEVERAGES

By comparison with other nationals, the people of the French-speaking Antilles seem abstemious. Among the country folk, a man will sit for hours, nursing his rum in the shade of his yard. Sometimes he will take off for the nearest *tonelle*, or palm-leaf-covered stand, where a *marchande* will offer him a stool and a glass of *trempe* or spiced rum for a coin and exchange gossip with him. The bottles on her stand bear no label. Against the sunlight they reveal, steeped in the raw white rum (with regional variations), anise leaves, cinnamon sticks, peppercorns, lime peel, and pineapple rind, selected for the circumstance, the state of digestion, or the day of the voodoo calendar. Stomachic, aphrodisiac, what you will, but always tasty.

Apéritif time, when it takes place in the best of circles, for an anniversary, a special holiday, or before a family dinner is, by tradition, a charming, conversational, seated affair where the beautiful women look their prettiest in decolleté dresses and heirloom jewelry of heavy gold. Some of the men will be courting them in words and phrases forgotten in fast-pace countries. The women, secure as a group, will be laughing softly, teasingly. In a corner by themselves some men will be talking business. The general tone of the conversation will never rise. After the second drink (of which the women never partake), the hostess will escort the guest of honor to the dining room, the others following. There will be a succession of dishes, each with the appropriate wines imported from France and semisweet champagne with dessert. After coffee will come cordials on the terrace in the sweet-smelling Caribbean night. The men's corner may slip into stories of the latest scandal, but the ladies, bless them, will only drape themselves more elegantly in their chairs until the evening comes to a restrained close.

The taste for cocktails runs sweeter in the Antilles than in the United States or even France. I have cut down on their sugar content. Sugar cane, from which rum is derived, came to the colonies with the Spaniards, who in turn had it from the Arabs, who had bought it in the markets of Calicut, whence it had come from China, where it was native. Sugar cane culture, introduced by the Jesuits, was an immediate success in the Caribbean area. The buccaneers and the filibusters who, after the Spaniards abandoned the islands, operated from the island of La Tortue, distilled a crude rum for their own use. The French planters who succeeded them improved this rum and soon exported it to the mother country, where it became part of military and naval rations.

In the early eighteenth century, when the punch craze spread from the Orient with the trading companies, rum and tropical fruit juices soon replaced the five original ingredients of punch in the ornate silver and fine Chinese porcelain bowls which the planters owned. Now, in elegant society, the rum highball is the men's choice.

Fruit Juice

Fruit such as papaya, pineapple, orange, or soursop, peeled and seeded
Crushed ice (optional)
Water
Sugar
Lime juice

1. Force fruit pulp through a very fine strainer, adding enough water for the proper drinking consistency; or process in an electric blender, adding ½ cup crushed ice per cup of pulp and enough water to dilute.
2. Add sugar and lime juice to taste. Serve chilled.

Fruit Punch

2 cups orange juice
2 cups pineapple juice
2 cups grapefruit juice
2 cups grenadine or
    1 small can frozen Samoa
    punch, thawed
1 cup papaya juice
  Sugar (optional)
  Ice block
2 bottles ginger beer, chilled

1. Mix juices and sweeten to taste. Chill.
2. Pour chilled ingredients over ice block in a punch bowl. Just before serving, add ginger beer.

Sugar Syrup

4 cups sugar
1 cup water

1. Combine sugar and water in a saucepan. Stir over low heat until sugar is dissolved. Reduce heat and simmer until liquid is clear (about 3 minutes).
2. Cool and use as needed. Store in a glass jar in refrigerator.

About 3¼ cups

Coconut Delight

2 cups Coconut Milk (page 86)
2 cups light rum
2 cups cracked ice
½ cup packed brown sugar
½ cup lime juice
  Coconut shells

1. Shake all ingredients well in a cocktail shaker, or process in an electric blender.
2. Serve in Coconut Shells along with straws.

Coconut Shells: Select small ripe coconuts. Remove the part with the 3 eyes with a saw. Smooth the outside of the nut with steel wool; remove as much fiber as possible. Rinse the coconut and serve with the flesh in the nut. To keep the shells for later use, place in the sun to dry out. Remove the loosened flesh. Rinse and dry. Store the shells.

Peach Rum

3 pounds peaches, halved, pitted, and sliced
4 cups packed brown sugar
  Grated peel of 1 lime
  Amber rum (about 6 cups)

1. Put ingredients into a 1-gallon container, using enough rum to fill.
2. Seal container and place on a sunny window sill, occasionally turning it.
3. After 3 months, pour off the liquor and serve in small cordial glasses.

Rum Punch

  Cracked ice
2 cups amber rum
¼ cup lime juice
2 jiggers grenadine
2 jiggers cane or maple syrup
1 jigger orgeat
5 dashes Angostura bitters

1. Half fill a pitcher with cracked ice and add ingredients.
2. Pour punch over cracked ice in highball glasses. Garnish with a stirrer of **peeled sugar cane**, if available.

Bishop's Punch

1 orange
25 cloves
4 cups amber rum
  Ice block
1 cup red port wine

1. Pierce orange and insert 1 clove at a time. Marinate in the rum overnight.
2. Pour the rum over ice block in a punch bowl; add port.
3. Slice the marinated orange; serve each cup of punch with ½ orange slice.

Latin-American Punch

1 bottle Rhine wine
1½ cups amber rum
1 cup lemon juice
1 cup orange juice
½ cup curaçao
16 fresh pineapple chunks
1 bottle champagne
2 cups club soda
1 ice block (1 quart)
  Flaked coconut

1. Mix wine, rum, lemon juice, orange juice, and curaçao, then add pineapple chunks. Chill 2 hours.
2. Pour chilled mixture, champagne, and soda over ice block in a large punch bowl.
3. Serve in chilled glasses or cups with coconut on top.

Pineapple Punch

1 large pineapple, cubed
1 cup cracked ice
¾ cup lime juice
¾ cup cherry brandy
¾ cup orgeat
  Ice block
1 cup sliced banana
2 limes, thinly sliced

1. Process pineapple, cracked ice, lime juice, brandy, and orgeat in an electric blender.
2. Pour over ice block in a punch bowl. Add sliced banana and lime. Stir well.
3. Ladle into cups.

Note: If a blender is not available, grate the pineapple and press in a sieve to extract the juice. Mix pineapple juice with cracked ice, lime juice, brandy, and orgeat in a pitcher.

Kenscoff Mulled Wine

1 bottle Burgundy
½ cup honey
4 orange slices, halved
6 whole cloves
1 cinnamon stick
1 cup amber rum
½ cup packed brown sugar

1. Combine wine, honey, orange, cloves, and cinnamon in a saucepan. Bring to a boil, stirring constantly. Pour into a heatproof punch bowl.
2. Place brown sugar in a small tea colander. Heat rum, ignite it, and pour, while flaming, over the sugar into the punch bowl. Serve at once.

Kenscoff Punch Bowl

4 cups lemon juice
3 cups orange juice
2 cups curaçao
2 cups Peach Rum (page 89)
1 cup grenadine
2 bottles amber rum
  Large ice block

1. Combine all ingredients except rum and ice block and store in refrigerator overnight.
2. Pour chilled mixture and rum over ice block in a punch bowl.

20 servings

Rum Alexander

Cracked ice
2 cups amber rum
½ cup crème de cacao
½ cup whipping cream

1. Half fill a 1-quart cocktail shaker with cracked ice. Add ingredients and shake well.
2. Pour into chilled cocktail glasses.

Rum Cassis

2 cups amber rum
⅔ cup blackberry brandy
Ice cubes
Club soda (optional)

Combine ingredients in a pitcher. Pour over ice cubes in old-fashioned glasses or in highball glasses, adding club soda to fill the glasses.

Note: For a sweeter drink, use crème de cassis instead of the brandy.

Rum Flip

1½ cups Barbancourt rum or other amber rum
½ cup Sugar Syrup (page 89)
6 eggs

1. Half fill a 1-quart cocktail shaker with cracked ice. Add ingredients and shake well.
2. Strain into cocktail glasses.
3. Garnish with **grated nutmeg**.

Rum-Lime Cocktail

Cracked ice
2 cups amber rum
½ cup lime juice
½ cup honey

1. Half fill a 1-quart cocktail shaker with cracked ice. Add ingredients and shake well.
2. Strain into chilled cocktail glasses. Garnish side of glass with a thin slice of **lime**.

Rum Mist

Very finely crushed ice
1½ jiggers amber rum
Strip of lime peel

1. Half fill an old-fashioned glass with crushed ice. Pour in rum. Allow condensation to appear on outside of the glass; place in freezer for 1 hour.
2. Add peel to glass before serving.

1 serving

Rum Sour

Cracked ice
2 cups amber rum
½ cup lime juice
¼ cup Sugar Syrup (page 89)

1. Half fill a 1-quart cocktail shaker with cracked ice. Add ingredients and shake well.
2. Strain into whiskey-sour glasses. Garnish each with a **maraschino cherry** and a **pineapple wedge**.

Rum Vermouth

Cracked ice
1½ cups amber rum
½ cup dry vermouth
½ cup sweet vermouth
½ cup orange juice

1. Half fill a 1-quart cocktail shaker with cracked ice. Add ingredients and shake well.
2. Strain into well-chilled cocktail glasses.

Between the Sheets

Cracked ice
1¼ cups amber rum
1¼ cups cognac
1¼ cups curaçao
¼ cup lime juice

1. Half fill a cocktail shaker with cracked ice. Add ingredients and shake well.
2. Strain into chilled cocktail glasses.

Buccaneer Cocktail

Cracked ice
1 cup light rum
1 cup orange juice
¼ cup grenadine

1. Half fill a 1-quart cocktail shaker with cracked ice. Add ingredients and shake well.
2. Strain into chilled champagne glasses. Garnish with orange half-slices, if desired.

Café Guede

2 cups amber rum, warmed
½ cup lightly packed brown sugar
4 cloves
Peel of ½ lime
Peel of ½ orange
4 cups strong coffee

1. Put rum, brown sugar, cloves, and peels into a heat-proof punch bowl. Stir with a ladle.
2. Remove a ladleful of rum mixture and ignite it. Pour it back into the bowl to set the rest of the rum aflame. Pour in coffee while still flaming.
3. Serve in demitasse cups with whipped cream, if desired.

Cocktail au Clairin

Cracked ice
2 cups light rum
½ cup cane or maple syrup
½ cup lime juice
¼ cup orgeat
2 egg whites

1. Half fill a 1-quart cocktail shaker with cracked ice. Add ingredients and shake well.
2. Strain into chilled cocktail glasses.

Daiquiri Gardere

Cracked ice
2 cups rum
½ cup lime juice
¼ cup Sugar Syrup (page 89)
1 egg white

1. Half fill a 1-quart cocktail shaker with cracked ice. Add ingredients and shake vigorously, or process in an electric blender 2 seconds.
2. Strain into chilled cocktail glasses.

White Satin Cocktail

2 cups Coconut Milk (page 86)
2 cups amber rum
⅔ cup half-and-half
⅔ cup cane or maple syrup
⅔ cup creme de cacao
Coconut Shells (page 89)

1. Shake ingredients well in a cocktail shaker or process in an electric blender.
2. Pour over cracked ice in Coconut Shells. Garnish with grated nutmeg.

White Velvet

Cracked ice
2 cups Barbancourt rum or other amber rum
1 can (14 ounces) sweetened condensed milk

1. Half fill a cocktail shaker with cracked ice. Add ingredients and shake well or process in an electric blender.
2. Pour into stemmed glasses.

Zombie

1 egg white, beaten
Brown sugar
Crushed ice
2 cups amber rum
½ cup pineapple juice
½ cup papaya juice
¼ cup lime juice
¼ cup cane or maple syrup
Amber rum (8 teaspoons)
Banana slices and pineapple sticks

1. Dip rims of 8 highball glasses in the egg white and then in brown sugar.
2. Half fill a 1-quart cocktail shaker with crushed ice. Add 2 cups rum, juices, and syrup and shake well.
3. Pour liquid, including ice, into the glasses.
4. Float 1 teaspoon amber rum on each drink. Garnish each with 3 banana slices and 1 pineapple stick.

INDEX